974.9
Ken

6493

W9-BJH-828

00476-X

974.9   Kent, Deborah
KEN   America the beautiful.
               New Jersey

HATHAWAY HIGH

AMERICA the BEAUTIFUL

NEW JERSEY

By Deborah Kent

Consultants

Abraham Resnick, Ed.D., Professor of Social Studies Education, Jersey City State College

Barbara A. Tamburo, Assistant Director of Education, New Jersey Historical Society, Newark

Robert L. Hillerich, Ph.D., Bowling Green State University, Bowling Green, Ohio

CHILDRENS PRESS®

CHICAGO

The Delaware and Raritan Canal at Millstone

Project Editor: Joan Downing
Assistant Editor: Shari Joffe
Design Director: Margrit Fiddle
Typesetting: Graphic Connections, Inc.
Engraving: Liberty Photoengraving

Library of Congress Cataloging-in-Publication Data

Kent, Deborah.
  America the beautiful. New Jersey.

  (America the beautiful state books)
  Includes index.
  Summary: Introduces the geography, history,
government, economy, industry, culture, historic sites,
and famous people of this very small but very diverse
state.
  1. New Jersey—Juvenile literature. [1. New Jersey]
I. Title. II. Series.
F134.3.K46 1987   974.9   87-9401
ISBN 0-516-00476-X

Winter in New Jersey

TABLE OF CONTENTS

Chapter 1

A WELL-KEPT SECRET

A WELL-KEPT SECRET

"The deal is that we campaign separately," said Colorado Senator Gary Hart, pointing to his wife. Hart, a 1984 presidential hopeful, went on, "That's the bad news. The good news for her is that she campaigns in California, and I campaign in New Jersey."

All over New Jersey, people cried out in angry protest. Once again, an outsider had dismissed their state as material for a joke. Many commentators feel that Hart's thoughtless quip cost him the New Jersey Democratic primary.

New Jersey is one of the smallest states in the nation. Throughout its history it has been dominated by its larger neighbors, New York and Pennsylvania. Since the days of vaudeville, when comedians tossed off one-liners about "Joizy," its image has been bruised and battered. For many out-of-staters, New Jersey is little more than a road from New York to Philadelphia. The thought of New Jersey calls to mind polluted rivers, blighted cities, and smoking factory towers.

But New Jerseyans have always known that their state is full of hidden surprises. It is one of the most heavily industrialized states, yet it contains the largest tract of undeveloped land between Boston and Washington, D.C.

By the mid 1970s, New Jerseyans began to take a growing pride in their state's achievements. Little by little, this new sense of identity has spread outward in what some have termed the "New Jersey Renaissance." In the 1980s, New Jersey is drawing tourists and businesses at a rate never seen before. The old image of "Joizy" is crumbling at last.

Chapter 2
THE LAND

THE LAND

"Familiarity with New Jersey breeds respect," wrote John T. Cunningham, a leading expert on the state's development. "Here there is diversity, here there is contrast."

GEOGRAPHY AND TOPOGRAPHY

When the first Europeans explored the Atlantic Coast, mapmakers mistook the area now known as New Jersey for an island—one reason it was named after the British Isle of Jersey. Technically, New Jersey is a peninsula—a long, narrow finger of land surrounded on three sides by water. The Hudson River comprises most of the state's northern border with New York. To the west and south, the Delaware River separates New Jersey from Pennsylvania and Delaware. The eastern shore faces the Atlantic Ocean.

With an area of 7,836 square miles (20,296 square kilometers), New Jersey is one of the smallest states in the nation, ranking forty-sixth in size. Only Delaware, Connecticut, Hawaii, and Rhode Island are smaller. New Jersey could fit into the state of Texas thirty-seven times.

At its greatest length, from High Point in Sussex County to the tip of Cape May, New Jersey measures 166 miles (267 kilometers). If roads covered this distance directly, it could be traveled in about two-and-a-half hours. At its narrowest point, in the mid-section

New Jersey's legacy of the great glacier includes fields of crumbled rock (above) and the sheer walls of the Palisades cliffs along the Hudson River (right).

of the state just south of Trenton and Asbury Park, New Jersey is only 32 miles (51 kilometers) wide.

Despite its small size, New Jersey offers a landscape of startling variety. As one travels from county to county, the face of the land changes constantly.

THE LEGACY OF THE GREAT GLACIER

Some twenty thousand years ago, the vast sheet of ice that geologists call the Wisconsin Glacier ground its way southward from the Arctic. Eventually, it buried much of the land that is now northern New Jersey. Nearly a mile (1.6 kilometers) thick in some places, the glacier crushed great chunks of mountains and pushed them before it on its journey. The ice reached as far as present-day Metuchen, near Perth Amboy and Trenton, before it began to melt and recede as slowly as it had come.

In its wake, the glacier left mounds and ridges of silt, crumbled rocks, and the huge boulders that today form the hills of northern New Jersey. The moving ice gouged pits that filled with water to become the glacial lakes of Morris and Sussex counties. It shifted the flow of rivers, leaving behind a patchwork of marshlands. It carved out new river gorges and created the sheer walls of the spectacular cliffs of the Palisades along the Hudson.

11

Ramapo Lake and Windbeam Mountain as seen from Ringwood State Park

Today, northern New Jersey is ribbed with low mountain chains—the Kittatinnies in the west, the Ramapos and the Watchungs farther east. The highest peak is High Point, which stands 1,803 feet (550 meters) high in the northwestern corner of the state. From its crown, hikers enjoy a view of New York, New Jersey, and, across the Delaware, Pennsylvania.

The southern two-thirds of the state, untouched by the glacier's shaping hand, consists of a rolling lowland seldom more than 100 feet (30 meters) above sea level. This region belongs to the Atlantic Coastal Plain, which stretches along the eastern seaboard from New York to Florida. The sharp geographical differences between northern and southern New Jersey have had dramatic effects upon the history and development of the state.

LAKES, RIVERS, AND WETLANDS

In the spring of 1680, two Dutch missionaries explored the forests of northern New Jersey with an Indian guide. In their

The Great Falls of the Passaic River at Paterson

journal they wrote: "After we had traveled a good three hours over the high hills we came to a rocky one wherein we heard the noise of the water; and clambering up to the top we saw the falls below us, a sight to be seen in order to observe the power and wonder of God." They were the first Europeans ever to look upon the splendor of the Great Falls of the Passaic River, where one billion gallons (nearly four billion liters) of water a day crash over a cliff seventy-seven feet (twenty-three meters) high. The mighty falls, as awesome today as they were in 1680, are yet another legacy of the great glacier.

The Hudson and the Delaware are the longest rivers that touch New Jersey's soil. The three main rivers lying wholly within the state are the Raritan, the Passaic, and the Hackensack. The longest of these is the Raritan, which flows south from Morris County to Raritan Bay.

Nearly 13 percent of New Jersey's land consists of marshes, or "wetlands." Among the most important of these are the Great Swamp of Morris County, the Hackensack Meadowlands, and the bogs and salt marshes of the Pinelands. These swamps were long

The Pineland bogs (above) are home to hundreds of bird and animal species. Most of the New Jersey shore is protected by a series of sandbars (right) and finger-shaped islands.

regarded as useless wasteland. But today scientists realize that they provide drainage that helps prevent flooding. The marshes are also a vital habitat for hundreds of bird and animal species.

Hundreds of lakes and ponds sparkle across northern New Jersey. Many, such as Green Pond and Sunfish Lake, are relics of the Ice Age. Other lakes have been formed artificially by the damming of rivers and streams. Lake Hopatcong is the largest lake lying entirely within the state. Every summer, New Jersey's lakes come alive with tourists eager to escape the heat and bustle of the cities.

THE SHORE AND THE PINELANDS

The Atlantic coast, known to New Jerseyans as "the shore," is another magnet for tourists. Most of the shore is protected from heavy seas by a series of sandbars and finger-shaped islands. Seawalls have been constructed at Seabright and in other areas where erosion has begun to wash away the beaches. The coast is ragged with shallow bays, coves, and inlets. Though the coastline is inhospitable to shipping, it is ideal for recreation. From Sandy

Hook to Cape May, New Jersey's shore is a 127-mile (204-kilometer) series of smooth, sandy beaches. Sand and sun are among New Jersey's major natural resources. The shore has given rise to such famous resorts as Atlantic City, Wildwood Crest, Long Branch, Asbury Park, and dozens of others.

A few miles inland from the shore is the region of southern New Jersey known as the Pine Barrens, or the Pinelands. The Pinelands is a sprawling wilderness of 1.3 million acres (.52 million hectares). It is the largest undeveloped area in the heavily industrialized region that stretches from Boston to Washington, D.C. Some 80 miles (129 kilometers) in length and 30 miles (48 kilometers) wide, the Pinelands covers about 20 percent of the state of New Jersey.

The Pinelands consists of bogs, salt marshes, and low, dense forests of scrub pine, oak, and cedar. Some sections are covered with "pygmy forests" of dwarf pine and oak that are less than eleven feet (three meters) tall.

Beneath the Pinelands, the earth is riddled with natural tunnels and caverns fed by deep, hidden springs. This vast underground reservoir is known to geologists as the Cohansey Aquifer. It is estimated that the Cohansey Aquifer contains 7 trillion gallons (27 trillion liters), making it the largest source of fresh water on the eastern seaboard.

CLIMATE

Compared with other northern states, New Jersey's climate is relatively mild. Ocean breezes fan the coast in the summer and warm it in the winter. Throughout the year, temperatures in South Jersey tend to be a few degrees higher than those in the north. In July, the average temperature is 76 degrees Fahrenheit

(24.4 degrees Celsius) in the south and 70 degrees Fahrenheit (21.1 degrees Celsius) in the north. In January, temperatures average 36 degrees Fahrenheit (2.2 degrees Celsius) in Cape May and 34 degrees Fahrenheit (1.1 degrees Celsius) in the northern mountains. Still, New Jersey is sometimes subject to extremes. The highest temperature in the state's history was 110 degrees Fahrenheit (43.3 degrees Celsius), recorded on July 7, 1936, at Runyon. On January 5, 1904, the mercury plunged to minus 34 degrees Fahrenheit (minus 37 degrees Celsius) at River Vale in Bergen County.

New Jersey receives about 46 inches (117 centimeters) of precipitation annually. Rainfall is distributed evenly throughout the state. Occasionally, however, the state is hit by severe droughts. In 1981, for example, in an effort to conserve water, many towns forbade residents to fill swimming pools or sprinkle lawns.

THE LAND AND ITS USES

When most outsiders think of New Jersey, they picture its teeming industrial cities. It is not widely known that farms and forests still cover two-thirds of New Jersey's land.

In parts of Burlington, Hunterdon, and Somerset counties, families can gaze from the windows of their condominiums and admire Holstein cattle grazing peacefully in the fields below. Because it is so close to heavily populated areas, and because it is so highly productive, New Jersey's farmland is some of the most valuable in the country. An acre (.4 hectares) of farmland sells for an average of $3,140 in New Jersey. In contrast, farmland in Wyoming sells for about $165 an acre (.4 hectares). Most New Jersey farms are small, averaging about 129 acres (52 hectares).

Though farming is less important than it once was, field crops such as hay, corn, soybeans, and wheat (left) are grown throughout the state.
The people of this urban state truly appreciate New Jersey's unspoiled natural areas such as virgin woods (right), fields, and marshland.

Ever since colonial days, New Jersey has been known as the Garden State. Today, farming is much less important to the state's economy than it once was. But New Jersey is still one of the nation's leading producers of tomatoes, blueberries, cranberries, spinach, and peaches. Field crops such as hay, corn, soybeans, and wheat are grown throughout the state.

Perhaps because they are hemmed in by urban centers on all sides, the people of New Jersey cherish the state's woods, fields, and marshes. Before the Meadowlands Sports Complex opened in East Rutherford in 1976, environmental groups made certain that a large portion of these wetlands would be preserved as a nature center and recreation area. Today, egrets and herons nest in the shadow of the vast parking lots that surround Giants Stadium. The preservation of the Hackensack Meadowlands is proof that in New Jersey, progress and conservation not only coexist, but enhance one another.

Chapter 3
THE PEOPLE

THE PEOPLE

"Goya, oh boya!"

Working from his office in Secaucus, New Jersey, Jose Unanue selected this as the new slogan for his company, Goya Foods. For more than fifty years, Goya had sold Puerto Rican and Caribbean delicacies to the Hispanic community through small stores in the New York metropolitan area. But in the late 1970s, Goya began to branch out. Unanue discovered that not only Puerto Rican people have a taste for *caramales* and *candules*. His specialized line of ethnic foods now sells in major supermarkets all along the East Coast.

All over New Jersey, people like Jose Unanue draw upon their diverse backgrounds and talents, turning ideas into exciting new enterprises. Their inventiveness benefits not only New Jersey, but the nation as a whole.

THE CITY BELT

According to the 1980 census, New Jersey had 7,364,823 people, most of them living in urban areas. Although New Jersey is one of the smallest states in the union, it ranks first in population density—that is, the number of people per square mile or square kilometer. On the average, 940 people live on every square mile (363 on every square kilometer) of New Jersey's land. In contrast, only 9 people live on every square mile (3 people on every square kilometer) of land in South Dakota.

The residents of Carteret (below) are among the nearly five million New Jerseyans who live in the heavily industrialized region near Manhattan. Many people who live in these "bedroom" communities commute to Manhattan jobs via the George Washington Bridge (right).

Most of New Jersey's population is concentrated in two major metropolitan areas, one centering around New York City, and the other across the Delaware River from Philadelphia.

Nearly five million people—67 percent of all New Jerseyans— live in the heavily industrialized region within fifty miles (eighty kilometers) of Manhattan. Here, one town runs into the next without so much as a cornfield to divide them. Cities large and small are linked by a maze of highways, overpasses, and cloverleaf intersections that baffle out-of-state drivers.

Most of New Jersey's cities lie along the New Jersey
Turnpike (above) between Philadelphia and New York.

The second, smaller, metropolitan area extends along the
Delaware River from Trenton south to Camden. This, too, is a
region of heavy industry. The New Jersey towns near New York
and Philadelphia are sometimes referred to as "bedroom
communities" because so many of their residents commute to out-
of-state jobs, coming home only to sleep at night.

Benjamin Franklin once described New Jersey as "a cider barrel
tapped at both ends," a state whose human and natural resources
were drained by New York in the north and Philadelphia in the
south. Inevitably, New Jersey's position between these two giants
has affected the state's development. Today, nearly all of New
Jersey's major cities lie along a fifteen-mile- (twenty-four-
kilometer-) wide corridor from Philadelphia to New York,
roughly traced by the course of the New Jersey Turnpike. This
corridor, often called the City Belt, is the heart of New Jersey's
industry and business.

Beyond the City Belt, the population thins dramatically. Towns
are farther apart, separated by farms and quiet stretches of
woodland. In the heart of the Pinelands in southern New Jersey,
the population density drops to ten persons per square mile
(twenty-six persons per square kilometer). In population
distribution, as in so much else, New Jersey is a study in contrast.

The population of Hoboken (above), like that of many New Jersey cities, includes descendants of the early Dutch, Germans, Italians, Irish, and Poles, as well as blacks and Puerto Ricans.

ETHNIC NEW JERSEY

In 1723, a young couple from the Netherlands settled in the village of Middlebrook in central New Jersey's Somerset County. Altje and Christian van Doren had seventeen children, and by the time Altje died at the age of ninety-five, they had 352 direct descendants. Today, the van Doren family is still well-represented in and around Somerset County.

Throughout the state, family names survive as reminders of the original Dutch, British, German, and Swedish settlers. It is said that more descendants of the *Mayflower*'s Pilgrims live in Cape May than in all of Massachusetts.

Early in the nineteenth century, to the dismay of many long-time residents, New Jersey's ethnic makeup began to change. In the 1840s, thousands of Irish men and women fled to the United

States from a disastrous famine in their homeland. Many settled in New Jersey, where they worked to build the state's railroads and canals.

Shortly after the Civil War, Italians began immigrating to New Jersey as well. By the turn of the century, eastern Europeans were flocking to the humming factories in Hudson, Essex, and Passaic counties. During the two world wars, black people migrated from the rural south to work in New Jersey's war plants.

Today, virtually every ethnic group on earth can be found in New Jersey. Italian-Americans are the largest single group, accounting for some 35 percent of the total population. About 12 percent of New Jerseyans are black, and 6 percent are Hispanic.

Roman Catholicism is the most widely practiced religion in New Jersey. Most Protestant churches are also represented. About 6 percent of the people of New Jersey are Jewish.

Politically, New Jersey is divided almost evenly between Democrats and Republicans. New Jerseyans do not necessarily vote along party lines. In every presidential election from 1968 to 1984, New Jersey voted for the Republican candidate. But between 1950 and 1985, the voters chose only one Republican senator.

TRENDS OF THE EIGHTIES

The 1980 census showed a startling new trend in New Jersey's population distribution. Between 1970 and 1980, New Jersey's population increased only 2.7 percent, compared with the national average of 11.4 percent. As the number of jobs in heavy industry declined nationwide in the 1970s, people began to leave the manufacturing cities of northeastern New Jersey. Many headed to the "Sunbelt" states in the south and southwest where jobs were more plentiful.

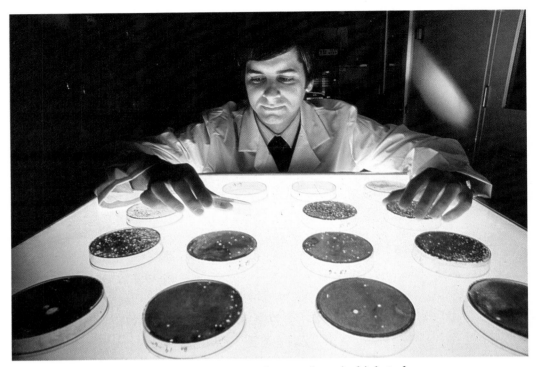

As jobs in heavy industry declined in New Jersey, those in high-tech industries such as pharmaceutical research (above) increased.

At the same time, new opportunities arose in research and computers—fields that rely on high technology. Seventy-five percent of the new jobs in New Jersey opened up in "high-tech" companies based in the previously rural northwestern counties. In the 1980s, journalists have described Morris, Somerset, and Middlesex counties as New Jersey's Sunbelt, comparing the boom in employment and population to the earlier boom in Texas.

Many young professionals, driven out of Manhattan by skyrocketing rents, have begun to renovate run-down houses along the Hudson River in cities such as Hoboken, Bayonne, and Jersey City. Once these waterfront towns glowered with miles of dingy slums, oil tanks, crumbling piers, and bridges. Today they are acquiring a new image. Luxury high-rises are springing up, and energetic new homeowners are restoring Victorian houses to their original splendor. As one news correspondent, formerly of

In Hudson River towns such as Fort Lee (right), young professionals are renovating run-down houses and developers are building luxury high-rises.

Manhattan, remarked, "I will no longer suffer in silence insults to Hoboken, land of my mortgage."

Southern New Jersey also has seen some unexpected changes. Real estate developers there are pioneering a new concept in housing for senior citizens. Scattered through the Pinelands are more than fifty retirement communities, their landscaped grounds blending into the surrounding forests. These adult communities offer golf courses, tennis courts, crafts studios, and heated swimming pools to retired people who wish to remain active and creative. More retirees choose to live in New Jersey retirement or adult communities than in any other northern state.

Chapter 4

THE GROWTH OF A COLONY

THE GROWTH OF A COLONY

The first people to reach the land we now call New Jersey arrived in scattered bands around 8000 B.C. They lived a nomadic life—hunting, fishing, and gathering wild fruits. By about A.D. 900 they began to plant corn, squash, and other crops, and to live in settled villages.

According to Professor Herbert Kraft of Seton Hall University, two distinct but related groups of native people lived in New Jersey before the coming of the Europeans. North of the Raritan River lived a people whose language was known as Munsee. The people who lived south of the Raritan called themselves the Lenape, a term that meant "ordinary people." For convenience, the name Lenape generally refers to all of New Jersey's native people.

THE ORDINARY PEOPLE

According to Lenape beliefs, the land and all of its resources were gifts from the creator. They could not be owned by any individual or group of people, but should be used by all with respect and care. The Lenape men hunted deer, bear, and turkeys with bows and arrows, and set nets across streams to catch fish. The women cared for the children and tended the fields. The Lenape traced their lineage through the families of their mothers and grandmothers rather than through their fathers' ancestors.

The Great Falls of the Passaic River as it looked in the eighteenth century

The Lenape were a fun-loving people, fond of music, storytelling, and games. They loved to watch the young men try to outdo each other in feats of strength such as lifting and throwing heavy stones. In one game, squares of bone painted on one side were tossed into a pottery bowl. The score depended on the number of squares that fell painted side up.

The Lenape traveled overland along a sprawling web of trails that crisscrossed their territory. On rivers and lakes they used dugout canoes, some of them as much as fifty feet (fifteen meters) long and holding twenty people.

The Lenape were fierce fighters when attacked, but most of the time they lived in peace with their neighbors. However, life was full of hardships. When game was scarce, or when the corn and squash withered in a drought, the village went hungry. The uncertainty of existence was summed up in the Lenape phrase for "good morning." Translated literally, it means "I'm glad you lived until morning."

In 1524, Italian navigator Giovanni da Verrazano became the first European to explore a portion of the New Jersey coast.

THE COMING OF THE WHITE MEN

In 1524, Italian navigator Giovanni da Verrazano anchored off the tip of Sandy Hook on the southern rim of Newark Bay. Setting out in longboats with a party of his men, he became the first European to explore a portion of the New Jersey coast.

New Jersey was not visited by white men again for nearly a century. In 1609, English explorer Henry Hudson, employed by the Dutch East India Company, sailed his ship the *Half Moon* into Newark Bay before he embarked on his famous voyage up the river that now bears his name.

When Hudson returned to Amsterdam, he reported that the land he had seen was full of promise. The woods teemed with fox, otter, mink, and beaver, and their pelts would fetch a fine price in European markets. Soon, bands of Dutch adventurers, eager to make their fortune in the fur trade, established their first trading post on the island of Manhattan. From this base they launched exploring and trading expeditions into New Jersey. The year 1618 marked the first European settlement in New Jersey—the Dutch trading post at Bergen. It was followed in 1630 by a settlement at Pavonia, now Jersey City.

In 1609, English explorer Henry Hudson sailed his ship the *Half Moon* into Newark Bay before sailing up what is now the Hudson River.

The Dutch were discovering southern New Jersey as well. In 1614, Captain Cornelius Mey sailed around New Jersey's southernmost tip. He is still remembered in its name today—Cape May. In 1623, Mey established Fort Nassau on the Delaware River near the present town of Gloucester.

The Dutch traders found that the Lenape, whom they renamed the Delaware, were peaceful and eager to exchange animal skins for iron kettles, muskets, blankets, and rum. The white settlements were small, and posed little threat to the Indians. But along with kettles and blankets, the Europeans brought smallpox, measles, and a host of other diseases never before known in the New World. The Lenape had no immunity to these illnesses, and terrible epidemics ravaged their villages. With the coming of the traders, their way of life was changed forever.

The Dutch were content to set up trading posts and small, scattered settlements. The British, however, were more ambitious. They wanted to establish strong, productive colonies that would enhance the wealth and glory of the king's realm. In 1664, the English king, Charles II, granted the Dutch domain in the New World to his brother James, duke of York. Without firing a shot, an English naval expedition took possession of Manhattan and the nearby Dutch holdings. The duke gave his own name to the larger of the two colonies, calling it New York. He named the smaller colony across the river for the island that had sheltered him during the bloody English civil war. The land between the Hudson, the Delaware, and the sea would thereafter be called New Jersey.

TROUBLE BETWEEN NEIGHBORS

The duke of York appointed Richard Nicolls to be the first governor of New York, and almost as an afterthought, put him in charge of New Jersey as well. A year later, apparently forgetting Nicolls, the duke gave New Jersey as a gift to two of his friends, Lord John Berkeley and Sir George Carteret. Governor Nicolls, naturally, was indignant. The duke tried to appease him by giving Staten Island, previously part of New Jersey, to New York. Thus, as early as colonial days, were sown the seeds of early tension between the states that face each other across the Hudson River.

Berkeley and Carteret divided New Jersey into two colonies, East and West Jersey. Strife continued to reign between the Jerseys and New York. In 1679, New York's governor, Sir Edmund Andros, insisted that New Jersey was still part of his territory, and should pay import duties to New York on goods from Europe. Philip Carteret, East Jersey's governor, swore that his people

When Philip Carteret refused to pay import duties to New York, soldiers dragged Carteret out of bed, savagely beat him, and hauled him away to New York in his nightshirt.

would never pay a penny. Enraged, Andros sent soldiers to Elizabethtown, the capital of East Jersey. They dragged Carteret out of bed, kicking and beating him savagely, and hauled him to New York, still dressed in his nightshirt. Finally, the king ruled against Andros and had him recalled. But Philip Carteret never recovered. He died in 1682, a broken, disillusioned man, at the age of forty-four.

New Jersey remained divided until 1738, when Lewis Morris of Monmouth County became the first royal governor of a united New Jersey. At last, after nearly seventy-five years, the British Crown had made it clear that New York had no power to dictate to New Jersey.

COLONIAL LIFE

Under British rule, settlement in the colony mushroomed. Almost immediately, families began to emigrate from New England and Long Island, lured by promises of religious freedom and inexpensive land. Within a few years, Newark, Bergen, Elizabethtown, Middletown, and Shrewsbury were thriving towns. Led by William Penn, the famous founder of Philadelphia, Quakers established settlements along the New Jersey side of the Delaware River.

The influence of New England Puritanism was reflected in the laws of colonial New Jersey. Swearing and drunkenness were penal offenses, with the stocks and the whipping post as popular forms of punishment. The death penalty was called for in cases of murder and witchcraft and for a thief's third offense. It also could be invoked against a child who cursed or struck a parent.

As early as the colonial period, New Jersey gained its reputation as the Garden State. On the rich soil of central New Jersey, corn grew 8 feet (2.4 meters) tall. Hunterdon County was sometimes called the state's bread basket because it produced more wheat than any other county in the colonies. Though much of this produce was sold locally, a large portion was grown for sale to the ever-hungry markets in New York and Philadelphia.

In order to haul its grain to the cities, New Jersey built a network of roads, many of them following old Indian trails. By 1765, New Jersey had more roads than any other British colony. Goods were carried to New York and Philadelphia in huge, cloth-topped "Jersey wagons," pulled by teams of four or six horses. The Jersey wagon, developed in the 1730s, is considered the first vehicle invented in America.

Not all New Jerseyans were farmers. Newark was known for its

In the 1700s, glassmaking arose as an important industry in Salem County. Some of the antique glass displayed in this Waterloo Village window may have been made during Colonial times.

tanneries and fine leather goods, and glassmaking arose as an important industry in Salem County. In the Kittatinny Mountains, miners excavated copper and iron ore.

Some families in New Jersey were immensely wealthy, building luxurious mansions with enormous private grounds. New Jersey also had its share of poor people, most of whom lived in the Pinelands and along the Delaware. And by 1760, the colony had some eight thousand black slaves. Overall, however, the people of New Jersey were members of the middle class. As Governor Jonathan Belcher remarked in 1748, New Jersey was the "best country I have seen for middling fortunes and for people who have to live by the sweat of their brows."

Chapter 5

JOURNEY INTO STATEHOOD

JOURNEY INTO STATEHOOD

"Whoever draws his sword against his prince must fling away the scabbard," wrote William Livingston, general of the New Jersey Militia in 1776. For decades, the gap between the colonies and the mother country had been widening. The colonists resented the burden of taxes demanded by the British king, and argued for a voice in their own government. At last, delegates from each of the colonies met in Philadelphia and signed the Declaration of Independence. There was no turning back now. The American Revolution had begun, and New Jersey was at war.

THE CROSSROADS OF THE REVOLUTION

While General George Washington strove to organize and train the Continental army, New Jersey was torn by internal strife. At the beginning of the revolutionary war, about half of New Jersey's citizens were still loyal to the king. These Loyalists, or Tories, burned and looted the homes of neighbors who had taken up the rebel cause. In turn, rebels burned the homes of real or supposed Tories.

Though the farm boys and villagers recruited for the New Jersey Militia were enthusiastic at first, they lacked training and discipline. Within a few months, most of the troops grew weary of army life. When their furloughs came up, many men went home and failed to report back to camp.

This painting by Emanuel Leutze depicts George Washington and his army crossing the Delaware River on Christmas night, 1776, as they prepared to surprise the Hessian soldiers in the British garrison at Trenton.

The British set up one of their key garrisons at Trenton, manning it with Hessian troops—German mercenaries (hired soldiers). On Christmas 1776, the Hessians threw themselves into a rollicking party, confident they had nothing to fear from the ragtag colonial army.

Late on Christmas night, the Hessian soldiers were awakened by a commotion outside. Having led his army across the Delaware River from Pennsylvania, General George Washington took the garrison at Trenton totally by surprise. Bleary with too much to eat and drink, the Hessians staggered from their bunks and groped for their weapons while the American rebels overran the fort. The battle was brief and decisive. Within a few hours, the Americans were in command of Trenton. The taste of victory

The Hessians captured by Washington were housed in the Old Barracks in Trenton.

revived the flagging spirits of the Continental army. The Battle of Trenton was the most important battle fought in the early years of the war.

American morale rose even higher a week later when Washington marched his troops out of Trenton and drove the British from Princeton, fifteen miles (twenty-four kilometers) away. The disgruntled British abandoned most of their strongholds in the state.

New Jersey's strategic position between Philadelphia and New York made it the site of almost constant activity during the Revolution. Some ninety engagements with the British were fought on New Jersey's soil. In the course of the war, George Washington spent about one-fourth of his time in the state, and today New Jersey towns are dotted with reminders that "Washington slept here." The abundant harvests of New Jersey farms helped to feed the Continental army. Iron ore from mines at Hibernia and Mount Hope in the north and Batsto in the south provided everything from shovels to cannons. It is little wonder that New Jersey has often been called the "Crossroads of the Revolution."

A reenactment of the January 3, 1777, Battle of Princeton

THE LONG ROAD TO VICTORY

Even after the victories at Trenton and Princeton, New Jersey was torn by strife between its Loyalist and rebel factions. William Livingston, who became governor in 1776, finally provided the leadership that was so desperately needed. In 1777 he created the Council of Safety, appointing himself as its head. The council forced all suspected Tories to take an oath of allegiance to the American cause. It tried hundreds of active Tories for high treason. Many were hanged, and their wives and children were deported in disgrace to other colonies.

Infuriated, the British offered a reward of one hundred pounds for Livingston's capture. Before the war was over, four attempts were made on his life. To evade capture, and to learn firsthand what was happening throughout the state, Livingston traveled ceaselessly. He never slept two nights in a row beneath the same

Some of the huts at Jockey Hollow, where Washington's soldiers spent the miserable winter of 1779-80, have been reconstructed.

roof. In 1780 he wrote, "My family for these four years past have not had fourteen days of my assistance."

Today most Americans know of the hardships endured by Washington's army during the winter of 1778-79 at Pennsylvania's Valley Forge. Though it has been nearly forgotten in the history books, the winter of 1779-80, when Washington encamped at Jockey Hollow outside Morristown, was perhaps harder still. Inflation was rampant in the warring colonies and the Continental army could not scrape together enough money to buy necessary provisions. A series of blizzards clogged the roads with snowdrifts as much as 12 feet (3.6 meters) deep. Half-starved and shivering in their ragged coats, the men marched through their maneuvers in boots riddled with holes. Washington wrote that his troops ate "every kind of horse food but hay."

Somehow the army survived Jockey Hollow. British resolve to cling to the colonies was steadily weakening. In 1781, the

American army set out from New Brunswick and marched south to victory in Virginia at the Battle of Yorktown. The tide of the war had turned. After six bitter years, the colonies at last had won their independence.

NEW JERSEY BECOMES A STATE

Though the colonies had cast off the British yoke, they had little sense of unity as a nation. For the first few years, the loose confederation of American states could not even agree on a location for its capital. At one point, Congress met in Trenton, and later convened briefly in Princeton.

In 1787, each of the former colonies sent delegates to the Constitutional Convention, which met in Philadelphia. By then, most American leaders realized that the new nation could not survive for long without a strong central government. At the same time, the special interests of each of the states must be protected. What sort of constitution could possibly satisfy everyone?

The delegates from New Jersey worried that the larger states, such as New York and Virginia, might become too powerful. They hastily proposed the "New Jersey Plan," by which all of the states would be represented equally.

Today each state sends congresspeople to the House of Representatives, the number being determined by the state's population. But the New Jersey Plan was adopted in the Senate. There, every state, large or small, is represented by two senators.

New Jersey had long worried about being dominated by her larger neighbors, but at last her fears were put to rest. Assured of an equal voice in the new federal government, New Jersey became the third state to ratify, or approve, the Constitution of the United States.

Chapter 6

INDUSTRY AND INVENTION

INDUSTRY AND INVENTION

Perhaps General Washington and his young colonel, Alexander Hamilton, were discussing strategy for the next battle with the British that July morning in 1778. But their talk must have come to an abrupt halt when they stopped at the base of the thundering Great Falls of the Passaic River.

Alexander Hamilton gazed in wonder, his imagination captured by the sight before him. When peace returned, the might of these spectacular falls could be harnessed for the benefit of humankind. Some day, he dreamed, the spot where he and General Washington now stood would lie at the heart of a splendid manufacturing city, a monument to the industry of a dynamic new nation.

THE SOCIETY FOR USEFUL MANUFACTURES

After the revolutionary war, New Jersey, like the rest of the United States, was chiefly a land of farmers. But Alexander Hamilton never forgot the city he had imagined at the foot of the Great Falls. In 1791, as secretary of the treasury, he set New Jersey on its course toward becoming a leading industrial state.

William Paterson, New Jersey's governor, eagerly authorized the funds to build a city at the Great Falls. The city would be run by a tax-free corporation called the Society for Useful Manufactures (SUM). The new city was named Paterson for the governor who brought it into being.

The Great Falls of the Passaic River (left) in Paterson provided water power for the manufacturing of textiles (above), locomotives, and heavy machinery.

Paterson got off to a slow start. In 1796, when an employee absconded with $50,000 in company funds, the SUM's only textile mill ground to a stop.

Alexander Hamilton never saw the pulsing hive of industry he had envisioned. On July 11, 1804, he met a political rival, Vice-President Aaron Burr, on New Jersey's famous dueling grounds at Weehawken. At Burr's first shot, Hamilton fell mortally wounded.

Yet Hamilton's dream city survived. When the War of 1812 cut off the supply of textiles from Great Britain, new Paterson mills opened. In 1836, Samuel Colt made his first Colt revolver in a Paterson factory, and the following year Paterson's first locomotive engine rolled out of the assembly plant. In the 1840s, silk replaced cotton cloth as the SUM's leading product, and for a century Paterson was known around the world as Silk City. The thundering falls of the Passaic River had fulfilled their promise.

By 1840, the Camden and Amboy Railroad spanned New Jersey to link Philadelphia with New York.

NEW JERSEY ON THE MOVE

Most of the goods produced by New Jersey's farms and mushrooming factories had to be shipped to New York or Philadelphia. As early as 1800, toll roads, or turnpikes, generated income for the state. By 1820, New Jersey had 550 miles (885 kilometers) of toll roads, more than could be found in any other state.

A series of stagecoach lines linked one New Jersey town to the next. Many carried passengers to the Hoboken Ferry, which in turn took them across the Hudson to their jobs in Manhattan. As early as the 1830s, some New Jerseyans were commuting to New York every day.

Stagecoach travel was tedious and uncomfortable. In 1800, one writer set down a list of satirical rules for coach passengers: "Let every man get in first with all his baggage and sit there firmly. . . . If any other complains that a trunk is too large for the inside, let him declare that it contains great value . . . and that it shall not go out. At every town let every man light a cigar and continue smoking in the face of his fellow travelers, and cursing the driver during each stage."

Soon the jouncing stagecoaches had to face competition. On May 12, 1825, the *New York Evening Post* announced, "Mr. [John] Stevens has at length put his steam carriage in motion. It traveled around the circle of the Hoboken Hotel yesterday at the rate of about 6 mph. . . . It will be in motion tomorrow from three o'clock until sundown." Hundreds of excited spectators flocked to view the miracle of the chugging horseless carriage. John Stevens's tiny circular track in Hoboken was the first operating railroad in America.

The Morris Canal, an astonishing feat of engineering, opened in 1831. Cutting 100 miles (161 kilometers) across New Jersey from Philipsburg to Newark, the canal carried Pennsylvania coal to cities all along its route. Ironically, the canal's success put it out of business. The slumping iron industry of Morris County revived when coal to run the smelting furnaces became plentiful. The ironworks made railroad tracks and parts for locomotives. When rail transport became widely available, the Morris Canal became obsolete.

By 1840, the Camden and Amboy Railroad, with a steamboat line at either end, spanned New Jersey to link Philadelphia with New York. The railroad was soon handling 450,000 passengers a year. Accidents were common. Sometimes the trains ran off the track, causing long delays. Passengers protested that their baggage was often damaged or lost, and that they were treated like "live lumber." But their complaints did little to improve the conditions. The Camden and Amboy Line drove out all competition and established a monopoly. For people who wanted to travel by train, there was only one line to choose.

Just as the horseless carriage was becoming a way of life, New Jerseyans greeted yet another astounding invention. Two bright young engineers, Alfred Vail and Samuel F. B. Morse, looped three miles (five kilometers) of wire around an iron forge in Morristown. On January 6, 1838, they tapped out a coded message with a primitive telegraph key: "A patient waiter is no loser." With those six simple words, New Jersey launched the world into the age of telecommunications.

INTO CIVIL WAR

Two headstones stand side by side in the Presbyterian churchyard in the New Jersey town of Springfield. The names on the stones read Elias Bryant Poole and William Quentin Poole. The Poole brothers lost their lives in the Civil War. William died fighting for the Union in the New Jersey Infantry; his brother Elias was killed while serving the Confederacy in the Little Artillery of Virginia.

At the end of the revolutionary war, there were some eleven thousand black slaves in New Jersey, more than in any other state in the North. About 25 percent of New Jersey's land lay south of Mason and Dixon's Line, the imaginary boundary between the North and the South.

Many New Jerseyans, especially the Quakers, passionately opposed slavery. An act passed in 1804 called for the gradual freeing of all slaves within the state. Quakers and free blacks helped thousands of runaway slaves escape from the South via the Underground Railroad, a secret system of "safe houses." Slaves were escorted through the state from one safe house to another.

Many New Jerseyans who opposed slavery helped thousands of runaway slaves escape from the South by way of the Underground Railroad, a secret system of "safe houses."

Despite some pro-Southern sentiment in the agricultural southern part of the state, New Jersey sent eighty-eight thousand troops to the Union army in the course of the war. The 33rd Regiment marched across Georgia with General William Tecumsah Sherman and suffered 60 percent casualties. Two of the Union's most important generals—Philip Kearny and George McClellan—were from New Jersey. Among New Jersey's war heroes was Willie McGee, a fifteen-year-old drummer boy from Newark. In 1863, he marched at the front of his regiment in a charge on a Confederate battery in Tennessee. For his outstanding bravery, Willie McGee was presented with the Medal of Honor.

No Civil War battles were fought on New Jersey's soil. But New Jersey did more than its share to preserve the Union. When the South surrendered in 1865, New Jersey and the nation stepped forward into a new era of growth and discovery.

Chapter 7

NEW JERSEY COMES OF AGE

NEW JERSEY COMES OF AGE

By the middle of the nineteenth century, though agriculture still flourished, New Jersey was already a predominantly urban state. In the decades after the Civil War, more and more New Jerseyans left the farms and settled in towns and cities. The image of the Garden State faded as manufacturing played a growing role in the state's economy. To thousands of men and women, New Jersey's thriving industries brought undreamed-of prosperity.

But for countless others, the age of industrial growth meant exhausting labor, poverty, and a draining sense of powerlessness. The immigrants from Europe, and later the blacks of the inner cities, fought a ceaseless battle for justice and equality.

THE HUDDLED MASSES

In New York Harbor, only a few hundred yards from the shores of Jersey City, the Statue of Liberty holds her torch high. Since her unveiling in 1886, the great copper-clad figure of "Lady Liberty" has greeted newcomers to the United States. The inscription at the statue's base reads in part: "Give me your tired, your poor, your huddled masses yearning to breathe free . . ." To millions of immigrants seeing America for the first time, these words embodied hope for a better life.

In the mid-nineteenth century, the ethnic makeup of New Jersey began to change. The state had been settled chiefly by

Of the millions of Europeans who had immigrated to the United States by the turn of the century, thousands found jobs in New Jersey factories.

Protestants from England and northern Europe. Many were alarmed when, in the 1840s and 1850s, thousands of Irish Catholics fled from famine at home and flocked to New Jersey.

The alarm spiraled to panic when the Irish were followed by Italians, Poles, Czechs, and Russians. The tide of Europeans swelled in the 1870s and 1880s, and by the turn of the century it had become a flood. Thousands of newcomers with strange customs and languages found jobs in the whirring factories of Newark, Passaic, Jersey City, and Paterson.

Despite the statue's promise of welcome, the factories paid shockingly little. The safety conditions were often horrifying, and men, women, and even children worked as many as fourteen hours a day. One writer described the daily routine of twelve-year-old laborers in a Paterson silk mill: "They have to rise [before] dawn of day, consume their morning meal by candlelight and trudge to the mill to commence their labor [before] the rising of the sun. . . . Their labor terminates at what is called eight o'clock at night, but which is really . . . much nearer nine o'clock. They then take supper and then immediately retire to bed in order that they may rise early in the morning."

The children who toiled at the textile mills of Paterson and other New Jersey cities (left), helped factory owners such as Catholina Lambert grow rich. Lambert even built a private castle on a hill overlooking Paterson (right).

While children toiled at their looms, the factory owners grew rich. One silk manufacturer, Mr. Catholina Lambert, even built a private castle on Garrett Mountain, a hill overlooking Paterson.

All across the nation, workers organized to improve factory conditions. In 1913, the mill workers of Paterson, backed by the Communist-affiliated International Workers of the World (IWW), staged a massive strike. By today's standards, their demands seem more than reasonable—an eight-hour working day and a minimum wage of twelve dollars a week.

For five months, most of Paterson's textile mills shut down, and striking laborers burned several of them to the ground. Police patrols and gangs of strikers clashed in the streets, while the IWW fanned the flames of anger and hatred. "If the strike is not won," declared one IWW leader, "Paterson will be a howling wilderness."

Even at the end of the strike, silk tycoon Catholina Lambert proclaimed that he would never give up the right to fire a man simply because he did not like his face. Many mills finally made concessions to the workers, though few met all of their demands. The strikers won somewhat higher wages and shorter working

Woodrow Wilson, who promised to fight corruption and institute workers' compensation, won a landslide 1910 election to become New Jersey's governor.

hours. But most important, the strike awakened in the workers a sense that, standing together, they had real power.

While immigrant workers struggled for power in the factories, the government of New Jersey was being run by a notoriously corrupt political machine. Political "bosses" used bribery and vote fraud to guarantee that only *their* supporters and *their* candidates became mayors, assemblymen, or chiefs of police.

The people of New Jersey were eager for change. They rallied around Woodrow Wilson, the thoughtful, bespectacled former president of Princeton University, when he decided to run for governor in 1910. Wilson promised to attack the corruption of the bosses and to fight the monopolies held by the railroads and utility companies. He would institute workers' compensation to aid laborers injured on the job. With his reputation for unimpeachable honesty, Woodrow Wilson was like no candidate the New Jersey voters had seen before. He won the race for governor by a landslide.

As soon as he took office, Wilson implemented the reforms he had pledged in his campaign. He sponsored laws that cut down on voting violations. He limited the power of the utility companies. And he provided for workers' compensation. Wilson's reforms earned him national recognition. In 1912, he left New Jersey to become the twenty-eighth president of the United States.

When the United States entered World War I in 1917, Hoboken became a major point of embarkation for soldiers on their way to France.

In 1914, Europe exploded in the horrifying madness of the greatest war the world had ever known. President Wilson was elected to a second term in 1916 largely because he pledged to keep America out of the European conflict. But this time he could not fulfill his promise. In 1917, half a million American soldiers, destined for the battlefields of France, steamed away from the docks at Hoboken. For the forty thousand young men who never returned, the Hoboken waterfront was their last glimpse of the United States.

POLITICAL MACHINERY

One of Wilson's most vocal supporters was Frank Hague, a young Irish police officer from Jersey City. In 1913, Hague was elected Jersey City's police commissioner. He immediately launched an all-out assault against corruption on the force. In a single day, he put 125 patrolmen on trial for violating regulations. As fast as policemen were fired, Hague replaced them with his own loyal supporters.

Hague's achievements as police commissioner won him the Jersey City mayoral election in 1917. Once his position was secure, however, he turned his energies to building a vast political machine of his own. In ward elections within the city, his henchmen stuffed ballot boxes with the votes of residents who had moved away or had been dead for years. Officeholders were forced to contribute a percentage of their salaries to City Hall. A generous portion of these revenues found their way into Frank Hague's pockets. He also encouraged illegal off-track betting, taking a share of the profits.

Hague tried to retain the image that he was truly a man of the people. He rewarded his supporters with Christmas baskets, picnics, and trips to the beach. He also built a modern medical center that provided free care for his followers.

Within a decade, Hague controlled not only Jersey City and surrounding Hudson County, but much of the state government as well. His influence even reached to Washington. In 1933 he wrote to President Franklin Roosevelt: "Should the occasion ever arise when New Jersey need be counted, I am yours to command."

DEPRESSION AND WAR

In the 1930s, the nation staggered under the most devastating economic depression in its history. The mills of Paterson and the factories of Camden, Newark, and Passaic closed their doors. Men and women who had worked all their lives now stood in soup-kitchen lines. Thousands lost all of their savings, even their homes.

It took the tragedy of the Second World War to put the American people back to work. While German tanks rumbled across Poland, the United States readied itself to enter the conflict.

'Any Rags—Old Clothes—'

The Jersey city political machine of Frank Hague (above) suffered a resounding defeat in 1949, an event noted by *Chicago Sun-Times* political cartoonist Jacob Burck (left).

As early as 1940, some New Jersey factory whistles were blowing again. The pace grew faster as the war effort stepped up. Shifts took turns around the clock. Factory owners sent out a call for more workers, and thousands of black people fled the poverty of the rural south to find jobs in New Jersey's cities. Instead of silk shirts, Paterson turned out army fatigues. Mighty destroyers steamed from the shipyards at Camden and Kearny. Fort Dix, Fort Monmouth, and Fort Hancock expanded and became important military bases. With relentless energy, New Jersey flung itself into America's effort to win the war.

Frank "I Am the Law" Hague remained in office as mayor of Jersey City until 1947. Toward the end of his thirty-year reign, his great machine began to run down. Abandoned by most of his former supporters, he was shadowed by indictments and lawsuits. At his funeral, an elderly woman marched up and down outside the church carrying a hand-lettered sign that read: "God have mercy on his sinful, greedy soul."

The era of post-World War II prosperity in the United States didn't reach the black families who lived in New Jersey's inner cities.

THE TROUBLED CITIES

Some economists predicted that the nation would slide into another depression as soon as the war plants closed down. Instead, the United States entered an era of peacetime prosperity. New Jersey's factories once more produced canned goods, plastics, textiles, and electronic machinery. Through the 1950s and 1960s, New Jerseyans bought new cars, television sets, and furniture. The construction industry boomed as tracts of woodland were cleared to make way for suburban housing developments.

But the postwar prosperity did not reach the black families who lived in New Jersey's inner cities. Black children attended understaffed, poorly equipped schools. Their parents worked at low-paying jobs, or had no work at all. As more and more middle-class white families moved to the suburbs, the cities lost tax revenues. The schools, public transportation, sanitation, and other services began to erode.

Three years after the city of Newark erupted in a bloody street riot (left), citizens elected Kenneth Gibson (above) to replace their corrupt former mayor Hugh Addonizio.

By the mid-1960s, more than half of the people in Newark were black. Yet the city was run entirely by whites. Thousands of blacks found themselves without jobs, living in overcrowded, deteriorating apartments, with little hope of escape. In July 1967, their frustration erupted in a bloody street riot that left ten million dollars in property damage and cost twenty-one lives.

In 1970, the people of Newark elected Kenneth Gibson to replace their corrupt former mayor, Hugh Addonizio. Gibson was one of the first blacks to become mayor of a major city. He helped to bring in federal grants for education, job training, and public housing. During his administration, the crime rate leveled off and infant mortality declined. Gibson encouraged white families and businesses to stay in the city. He fostered a sense of pride among Newark's black citizens, and instilled in them a belief that they have a voice in their city's government. Since 1967, Newark has struggled toward a slow and often painful rebirth.

Not all Atlantic City property owners were willing to sell out to casino developers when the city legalized gambling.

THE NEW JERSEY RENAISSANCE

Though it was still known to the world as the site of the annual Miss America Pageant, Atlantic City had been declining since World War II. The old hotels fell into disrepair as tourists sought out vacation spots with more glitter and glamour. Then in 1976, after years of debate in the New Jersey legislature, Atlantic City opened its doors to casino gambling. Today, the gleaming hotels along the boardwalk offer fine food, shows by top performers, and the fascination of games of chance in which ordinary people can dream of hitting the jackpot.

Some fifty-two million people—25 percent of the nation's population—live near enough to reach Atlantic City on one tankful of gasoline. In 1985, Atlantic City drew thirty million

In the same year the casinos came to Atlantic City (left), the Meadowlands Sports Complex (above) opened in East Rutherford.

visitors, more than Las Vegas, New York City, or Disney World, making it America's leading tourist attraction.

Critics argue that gambling has made Atlantic City a stronghold for organized crime. Many long-time Atlantic City residents, especially poor people and senior citizens, have been driven out by soaring rents. But Atlantic City's enormous popularity has benefits, too. The boom created thirty thousand new jobs, and brings $112 million in taxes to the state treasury each year.

In the same year the first casino came to Atlantic City, the dazzling Meadowlands Sports Complex opened in East Rutherford. Over the years, the Meadowlands, an 18,000-acre (7,284-hectare) marsh along the Hackensack River, had become a vast dumping ground for garbage and factory wastes. Now the harness-racing track, the Brendan Byrne Arena for hockey and

Giants Stadium at the Meadowlands (right) is home field for both of the New York area's major-league football teams, the Giants and the Jets.

basketball, and the football stadium draw millions of spectators annually. The Meadowlands stadium is home field for both of the New York area's major-league football teams, the Giants and the Jets. The sprawling Meadowlands complex also includes some one hundred office buildings and hotels, bringing thousands of jobs to northeastern New Jersey.

Another change in the image of New Jersey is the explosive development of industries that depend on highly advanced technology. In the late 1970s, as the number of manufacturing jobs declined, thousands of new positions opened in computer technology, medical research, and product development. Most of the new firms involved in this work are based in the relatively rural northwestern counties.

Atlantic City, the Meadowlands, and the new "high-tech" businesses draw people from all over the country. New Jersey is proving that it is not merely a pathway from New York to Philadelphia, but a place for growth, invention, and positive change.

Yet even in the 1980s, the centuries-old conflict between New York and New Jersey sometimes flares to the surface. In November 1984, Congressman Frank Guarini, a Democrat from Jersey City, filed a suit against New York, arguing that Liberty and Ellis Islands rightfully belong to New Jersey. The islands were granted to New York in 1833, fifty-three years before the Statue of Liberty's dedication, and fifty-eight years before Ellis Island opened as the point of entry for immigrants from Europe. Guarini brought to light key documents indicating that the islands may have been New Jersey's property all along.

The controversy sparked some friendly and some not-so-friendly debate. For Congressman Guarini and many other New Jerseyans, the suit over the islands was a matter of the state's emerging sense of pride. "New York is the Big Apple, and New Jersey was the stepchild," the Congressman explained. "Now New Jersey is claiming its rightful place. It's not vengeance, it's getting what we feel is rightfully ours."

Chapter 8

GOVERNMENT AND THE ECONOMY

GOVERNMENT AND THE ECONOMY

Each year the people of New Jersey pay millions of dollars in property, sales, and income tax to the state government in Trenton. In return, the state provides an array of services including schools, libraries, museums, and public transportation. By electing officials and voting on bond issues, the people help to decide how tax money will be used. The government and the services it supports are known as the public sector because they are controlled by the public.

The term *private sector* refers to profit-making businesses controlled by individuals or corporations. The way people live in New Jersey is determined by the public and private sectors functioning side by side.

GOVERNMENT

Like the federal government in Washington, the government of the state of New Jersey is divided into three main branches. These are the legislative, or lawmaking branch; the judicial branch, which interprets the law; and the executive branch, or the office of the governor.

The state legislature has two sections, or houses. The upper house is called the senate, and the lower house is called the assembly. The people of New Jersey elect forty senators and eighty assemblymen to fashion the state's laws.

New Jersey's court system somewhat resembles a pyramid. At the base are the municipal courts located in most towns. A county court resides in the county seat of each of the twenty-one counties. Cases can be appealed through a system of superior courts all the way to the state supreme court in Trenton.

New Jersey's current constitution was ratified in 1947. It strengthened the executive branch of the state government, increasing the governor's term of office from three years to four. The governor may hold office for two consecutive terms. He appoints most of the state's key officials, including secretary of state, attorney general, and commissioners of education, health, banking, and labor.

New Jersey's first sales tax went into effect in 1966. In 1970, New Jersey became one of the first states to raise money by selling tickets for a weekly lottery. New Jerseyans began to pay state income tax for the first time in 1976.

EDUCATION

The first public schools in New Jersey opened in 1817. Today, all children in the state between the ages of six and sixteen are required by law to attend school. In 1985, New Jersey spent an average of $4,007 per student. Only Alaska, Wyoming, and the District of Columbia had a higher expenditure per child.

In the 1984-85 school year, 716,723 girls and boys were enrolled in the state's 1,788 elementary schools, and 412,500 students attended 405 secondary schools. New Jersey also has a strong system of parochial schools, most of them run by the Catholic church.

New Jersey has sixty-two schools for children with physical or mental disabilities. The number of special schools declines year by

Albert Einstein (left) found Princeton University a haven for work and study.
Nassau Hall (right) served as barracks and hospital during the revolutionary
war and in 1783 was the headquarters for the Continental Congress.

year, as more children with special needs are integrated into
regular classes. New Jersey was one of the first states to pioneer
the "mainstreaming" of disabled children. By the early 1950s,
blind children were encouraged to attend their neighborhood
public schools.

The white-haired, mustachioed figure of Albert Einstein, riding
his bicycle along the quiet streets, was a familiar sight around
Princeton University in the 1940s and 1950s. Einstein developed
his theory of the origin of the universe while working at
Princeton's Institute for Advanced Study. He is one of dozens of
writers, artists, and scientists who have found the intellectual
atmosphere of Princeton a haven for study and work.

Established in 1746, Princeton is the fourth-oldest university in
the country. Today, the school draws outstanding students from
every state in the union and from many foreign lands as well. In
Princeton's libraries, students have access to some three million
volumes occupying nearly 100 miles (161 kilometers) of shelf
space.

In the nearby city of New Brunswick stand the halls of Rutgers,

Murray Hall, on the Rutgers University College Avenue campus

New Jersey's state university. Chartered in 1766, Rutgers has enjoyed a friendly rivalry with Princeton for more than two centuries. In addition to the main campus, the university now has branches in Newark and Camden. Rutgers offers graduate degrees in law, medicine, management, and many other fields.

New Jersey's nine state colleges are Montclair, Trenton, Glassboro, Jersey City, Kean in Union, Stockton, Ramapo in Mahwah, William Paterson in Wayne Township, and the New Jersey Institute of Technology in Newark.

Other outstanding colleges and universities include Drew University in Madison, Fairleigh Dickinson University in Rutherford, Monmouth College in Long Branch, Saint Peter's College in Jersey City, Rider College in Lawrenceville, and the Stevens Institute of Technology in Hoboken.

TRANSPORTATION AND COMMUNICATION

As early as the 1700s, ferries shuttled goods and passengers back and forth across the Hudson and Delaware rivers. The ferries have been replaced by some of the busiest tunnels and bridges in the world. The George Washington Bridge arches over the Hudson to link Fort Lee on the Palisades with Upper Manhattan. Motorists can also reach New York via the Lincoln and Holland tunnels. The Benjamin Franklin Bridge spans the river between Camden and Philadelphia.

To millions who travel north and south along the eastern seaboard each year, New Jersey means the New Jersey Turnpike—that teeming, 118-mile (190-kilometer) highway that stretches across the state from New York to Philadelphia. As wide as a football field is long, the turnpike is the most heavily traveled tollway in the nation.

At one point in Newark, a traveler on the turnpike can take in a panorama of modern transportation at a single glance. A set of Conrail tracks parallels the highway on one side, while on the other, huge oceangoing ships steam into Newark's cargo port. Overhead roar giant jet planes from Newark International Airport, bound for destinations all over the globe.

New Jersey has 33,000 miles (53,097 kilometers) of roads and highways. Most important after the turnpike is the scenic Garden State Parkway, which runs from the New York State border along the shore to Cape May. New Jersey also has 1,650 miles (2,655 kilometers) of railroad track. Thousands of commuters still reach New York and Philadelphia every day by train.

Once praised for its lack of congestion, Newark Airport was referred to as the New York area's best-kept travel secret. The airport is constantly expanding to meet growing demands, however, and by 1987 had become one of the nation's busiest

Thomas Edison, an early communications pioneer, developed the phonograph at his Menlo Park laboratory in 1879.

airports. In 1986, even the grassy field where airport employees once played baseball was turned into a parking lot for jumbo jets.

Since Morse and Vail invented the telegraph in 1838, New Jersey has been a pioneer in the field of communications. The first radio signal was transmitted at Princeton in 1840. Thomas Edison, working at his "invention factory" in Menlo Park, developed the phonograph in 1879. He put the device aside as an interesting toy with few practical uses. In 1901, the Victor Talking Machine Company of Camden began to sell flat recorded disks and the machine to play them, known as the Victrola.

New Jersey's only VHF (very high frequency) television station is WOR, with broadcasting towers in Secaucus. Viewers were once limited to news and public affairs programs from and about New York and Philadelphia. Since the advent of cable television, however, stations have sprung up in Newark, Montclair, and several other cities, highlighting New Jersey news and programs of local interest.

Though the *New York Times* and *Philadelphia Inquirer* are widely read in New Jersey, the state has many fine newspapers of its own. The *Bergen Record*, the *Asbury Park Press*, the *Newark Star-Ledger*, and the *Camden Courier-Post* are among the most widely respected. New Jersey has 30 daily newspapers and 225 weeklies.

The chemical industry is one of the mainstays in New Jersey's economy. Chemical plants produce such things as drugs, plastics, paints, rubber, and a variety of cosmetics.

MANUFACTURING AND HIGH TECHNOLOGY

"I know all the jokes about New Jersey," native New Jerseyan Ed Rutsch told a writer from *National Geographic* magazine. "This place doesn't have to apologize. New Jersey produces, it hustles, it's tough."

With more than seven hundred thousand workers busy in some fifteen thousand manufacturing plants, New Jersey has been referred to as "the workshop of the nation." Heavy industry is concentrated in two major areas—along the Hudson River around Jersey City, Newark, and Elizabeth, and on the lower Delaware River between Trenton and Camden. New Jersey's factories produce everything from electronic machinery to clothing, from canned goods to fine china.

The chemical industry is one of the mainstays in New Jersey's economy. Chemical plants produce plastics, rubber, and a wide assortment of cosmetics. New Jersey leads the nation in the production of pharmaceuticals. The drug interferon, which may prove vital in the fight against cancer, was developed at the sprawling Hoffman LaRoche plant in Nutley.

In the late 1970s, New Jersey's economic profile shifted. In Mahwah, a Ford assembly plant shut down, putting thousands of

New Jersey leads the nation
in the production of
pharmaceuticals.
Left: Pill production at the
Hoffman LaRoche plant in Clifton

employees out of work. The "smokestack industries" along the
Hudson began to slump. Automobiles and other goods were being
made more cheaply abroad, and many American companies could
not compete.

But as New Jersey lost manufacturing jobs, the number of jobs
in service industries nearly doubled, climbing from 410,400 in
1970 to 787,600 in 1985. The service industries include tourism
and recreation, retail and wholesale trade, finance, transportation,
and utilities. Many corporations, driven out of New York by high
rents and limited space for expansion, have moved their
headquarters to New Jersey.

New Jersey in the 1980s reflects a growing national trend away
from manufacturing and toward industries that rely on advanced
technology. These high-tech industries include research and
product development in computers, medicine, aerospace, and
telecommunications. By the mid-1980s, more than 10 percent of
all the research dollars in the country were being spent in New
Jersey.

This anechoic chamber, a nearly echo-free sound laboratory, is at Bell Labs, one of the most respected research firms in New Jersey.

One of the oldest and most respected research firms in the state is Bell Labs, with branches in Holmdel, Union, and Murray Hill. Scientists at Bell Labs helped to develop the laser, a highly concentrated light beam used in delicate surgery. Bell Labs also developed an "electronic brain" that guides American satellites as they spin through space.

The transition from manufacturing to high-tech industry is not an easy one, but New Jersey is proving equal to the challenge. "The climate for business has never been as good," commented a Rutgers economist in 1985. "New Jersey has moved from the tail end of the train to being one of the locomotives."

HAZARDOUS WASTES

For months Joe Reinhart pleaded with state officials, and for months his requests were ignored. No one would come to investigate the rumors of secret "midnight dumping." Finally,

Dangerous chemical wastes pose a nationwide problem. In industrial New Jersey it is especially severe, and the state works hard to minimize the dangers. Here the coast guard puts out a fire in an Elizabeth chemical dump.

Reinhart and a group of neighbors took the matter into their own hands. In December 1982, they began to dig in a pine grove 1,000 yards (914 meters) from Reinhart's home in Shamong Township. Within a few hours, they uncovered exactly what they feared they would find. Two feet (.609 meters) down, their shovels struck a 55-gallon (208-liter) chemical storage drum. Joe Reinhart was living beside a hazardous waste dump.

New Jersey's factories and chemical plants create jobs for millions of people and produce goods that the nation craves. But a tragic by-product of industry is pollution. As early as the 1890s, companies in New Jersey, as well as many in New York and Pennsylvania, began to dump their refuse in New Jersey's woods and marshes. When laws were enacted to try to regulate this practice, illegal "midnight dumpers" got into the waste-disposal business. Much of this industrial waste contains chemicals that are poisonous to animals, plant life, and human beings.

Dangerous chemical wastes pose a nationwide problem. But in New Jersey, it is especially severe. The federal Environmental Protection Agency (EPA) gave clean-up priority to ninety-seven major dump sites in New Jersey, more than it identified in any other state.

Not content to wait for help from the federal government, New Jersey created its own clean-up fund by passing a $100-million

Though agriculture is less important in New Jersey than it used to be, about 21 percent of the land is used for farming of one kind or another.

bond issue in 1981. The state's tough Environmental Clean-up Responsibility Act requires companies to remove safely all pollutants before closing down or selling their property. Yet, as one state official laments, "There are no easy solutions . . . absolutely none. . . . People want to believe that you can correct a problem that took a hundred years to develop in a week and a half."

AGRICULTURE

In December 1985, Ted and Susan Blew sat before a desk at the Hunterdon County Courthouse in Flemington, signing their names to a stack of official-looking documents. When the final papers had been exchanged, cameras flashed and a cheer rose from the small crowd of witnesses. The Blews were the first New Jersey farmers to sell the development rights to their land under the State Farmland Preservation Program. By this act, they guaranteed that their 160-acre (64.7-hectare) farm in Franklin Township will be preserved permanently solely for agriculture.

Apple trees are in bloom at this Mercer County farm (left) that specializes in the production of apples and peaches. New Jersey is the second most important producer of blueberries (right) in the country.

Today, agriculture accounts for only 2 percent of the goods produced in New Jersey each year. But the Garden State is still deeply committed to farming. Some 21 percent of the state's land is devoted to orchards, dairies, truck farms, and nurseries.

The rich, loamy soil of central and southern New Jersey is ideal for raising vegetables and fruits. New Jersey is the fourth most important producer of tomatoes in the country. In blueberries and cranberries, grown in the bogs of the Pinelands, New Jersey ranks second and third, respectively. New Jersey peach and apple orchards yield an abundant harvest every fall. Other important products are spinach, asparagus, squash, melons, and pumpkins.

The stony soil of northern New Jersey is less conducive to crop production. Instead, the farmers of Sussex, Warren, and Hunterdon counties raise poultry and dairy cattle. Hilly Somerset County is famous for beautiful thoroughbred horses.

Year by year, real estate developers and expanding businesses encroach on New Jersey's farmland, some of the most valuable in the nation. But thousands of New Jersey farmers like Ted and Susan Blew are determined to keep the Garden State green.

Chapter 9

CULTURE AND RECREATION

CULTURE AND RECREATION

The people of New Jersey have always worked hard. But recreation and cultural activities are important, too. No understanding of the state would be complete without examining the ways New Jerseyans fill their leisure hours, and the contributions they have made to the cultural life of the nation.

FOLKLORE

Before public education was widespread, few people in the colonies knew how to read or write. In the absence of books, movies, or television, New Jersey families passed long winter evenings by telling stories around the kitchen fire. Many of these stories, layers of fantasy heaped upon some forgotten kernel of truth, evolved into legends that are still retold and half-believed in rural areas today.

The most famous New Jersey legend tells of the "New Jersey Devil" of Atlantic County. Expecting her thirteenth child, Mrs. Leeds of the town of Estelville exclaimed in a thoughtless moment that she would rather have a devil than another baby. When her child was born it had a long tail, cloven hoofs, the face of a horse, and the wings of a bat. It flew out the window and settled in a nearby swamp; even today, it is said to enjoy startling the unwary hunter or hiker. The New Jersey Devil is allegedly harmless, though he takes an active interest in human affairs. One Atlantic County judge claimed to have breakfast with the Devil every

According to New Jersey folklore, the bloodthirsty pirate Blackbeard buried a fabulous treasure of gold and jewels beneath a walnut tree in Burlington.

morning, discussing politics with him over ham and eggs. The legend received national attention when a state hockey team adopted the name "New Jersey Devils."

Tales of buried treasure are prominent in New Jersey's folklore. The bloodthirsty pirate Blackbeard is said to have buried a fabulous cache of gold and jewels beneath a walnut tree in Burlington. One of Blackbeard's comrades, a Spaniard, was stabbed and buried upright to guard the treasure chest. According to some Burlington residents, the ghost of the Spaniard's big black dog still prowls the streets on moonless nights.

Another legendary treasure was hidden in a Gloucester County sand pit by slaves escaping on the Underground Railroad. A phantom rabbit digs a new hiding place whenever the gold is threatened. Someday, the story goes, the treasure will be discovered by the descendants of slaves at a time when the black race is in dire need.

81

LITERATURE

The earliest literary figure to emerge in New Jersey was John
Woolman, a traveling Quaker preacher. His vivid *Journal*,
published in 1774, is regarded as one of the most important
records of everyday colonial life. Woolman was among the first
Americans to write passionately against the evils of slavery, and
he provided a spiritual foundation for the abolition movement.

The writing of poet Philip Freneau also was inspired by the
political issues of his time. George Washington once denounced
him as "that rascal Freneau" because of his outspoken support of
the French Revolution. His long poem "The British Prison Ship"
recounts his capture during the revolutionary war. Some critics
consider Freneau the first poet of genuine merit to emerge in the
United States.

Many authors famous for their writing about other parts of the
country drew on the years they spent in New Jersey. Washington
Irving, usually associated with "The Legend of Sleepy Hollow"
and other tales of the settlers along the Hudson in New York,
lived in Newark from 1806 to 1807. He wrote a series of poems
about the Passaic River and the surrounding countryside. Stephen
Crane, born in Newark, is sometimes called the "father of the
American psychological novel." Crane's masterpiece, *The Red
Badge of Courage*, is a riveting novel about the Civil War. One of
his less-well-known works, *The Whilomville Stories*, is a portrait of
New Jersey village life.

The literary scene was fairly quiet in New Jersey until the late
nineteenth century. In 1873, Walt Whitman, already well
established as a journalist and poet, went to Camden to convalesce
after a stroke. Whitman's home was a magnet for dozens of
writers and artists who criticized and stimulated one another's

Among the famous authors who lived for a time in New Jersey are Walt Whitman (above) and Washington Irving. Irving is usually associated with "The Legend of Sleepy Hollow" (right), but he also wrote a series of poems about the Passaic River and the surrounding countryside.

work. Some of Whitman's finest poetry was written during his Camden years, including major revisions of his celebrated collection *Leaves of Grass*.

For fifty years, physician William Carlos Williams practiced as a pediatrician in Rutherford. When he wasn't treating chickenpox or removing tonsils, Williams wrote poetry. His masterpiece, "Paterson," is considered by some critics to be America's greatest epic poem. The poet traced the story of the Great Falls from untouched wilderness to

> . . . the modern town,
> disembodied roar! the cataract and
> its clamor broken apart; — and from
> all learning, the empty
> ear, struck from within, roaring . . .

These examples of early American glass at the Wheaton Museum of American Glass were made at the time of master craftsman Casper Wistar.

Williams died in 1963, the year he won the Pulitzer Prize. He is only one of more than twenty New Jersey writers who have received the coveted Pulitzer Prize for their literary achievements. Others include historian Will Durant, for his monumental eleven-volume *The Story of Civilization*, and noted critic Van Wyck Brooks for his treatise on American literature.

FINE ARTS AND CRAFTS

During the colonial period, few New Jerseyans had time for painting or sculpture. But many found artistic expression as they created objects that were both practical and beautiful. Casper Wistar studied glassmaking under master craftsmen from the Netherlands. Using quartz crystals from deposits in South Jersey, he added a fresh New World flavor to the European tradition. By 1750, the glassworks at Wistarburg was highly regarded throughout the colonies. The seven Stanger brothers studied under Wistar before they opened a glassworks of their own in 1775. They are still remembered in the name of the town they helped to establish, Glassboro. Today, collectors pay handsome

"The Brook, Montclair," is one of the many New Jersey landscapes
painted by artist George Inness during the time he lived in Montclair.

prices for bottles and bowls of early New Jersey glass. Glassware
is still produced in Glassboro and throughout Salem County.

The first New Jersey artist to gain recognition was a remarkable
woman from Bordentown named Patience Lovell Wright. As a
young widow with three small children, Wright traveled to
England in 1772 to seek her fortune as a sculptress. She was a
close friend of Benjamin Franklin, and some historians suspect
that she acted as an American spy during the revolutionary war.
At a time when art was considered a most unsuitable profession
for a woman, her work was well received. Her full-length wax
portrait of British statesman Sir William Pitt still stands in
Westminster Abbey. Wright was the first American artist to be so
highly honored.

By the mid-nineteenth century, America had established its own
artistic tradition. George Inness, who spent many years in
Montclair, was one of America's foremost landscape painters.

Some of his works were inspired by the hills overlooking the Delaware River. He also painted many scenes of the woods and fields around Montclair.

In the 1970s and 1980s, art colonies sprang up in Hoboken, Jersey City, Newark, and Paterson. Artists converted empty warehouses into studios full of light and color. With some thirty thousand painters and sculptors living and working in the state, New Jersey's artistic tradition continues to thrive.

ENTERTAINMENT

Soon after the turn of the century, Thomas Edison, working at his laboratory in West Orange, developed the first motion-picture camera. From 1907 until 1917, Fort Lee was the capital of the dazzling new movie industry. Mary Pickford, shining star of the silent screen, had her debut in the 1909 film *The Violin-maker of Cremona*. Pearl White starred in the serialized *Perils of Pauline*. The last moments of one episode saw her dangling by her fingertips from the Palisades high above the Hudson. The scene left viewers in such heart-racing suspense that it bequeathed a new term to our language. Today a tensely dramatic scene that is left unresolved is still referred to as a "cliff-hanger."

One of the first New Jersey performers to win international acclaim was Paul Robeson. Born in Princeton in 1898, Robeson was the son of a former slave. He attended Rutgers University, where he starred on the football team. After graduating at the head of his class, Robeson obtained a law degree from Columbia. Because widespread discrimination against black people prevented him from establishing a legal practice, he turned his energies to another profession, acting. Robeson starred in *The Emperor Jones*, *Othello*, *Show Boat*, and many other plays. He became famous for

During the time Fort Lee was the capital of the movie industry, Pearl White starred in the serialized *Perils of Pauline* (above). Paul Robeson, one of the first New Jersey performers to win international acclaim, starred in many plays, including *Othello, Show Boat,* and *The Emperor Jones* (below).

Two of New Jersey's most famous entertainers are Frank Sinatra, surrounded by teenaged fans in 1943 (above), and Bruce Springsteen (right).

his rich baritone singing voice, and interpreted black spirituals with feeling and dignity.

New Jersey's nightclubs have given many talented performers the start they needed. William "Count" Basie of Red Bank organized his first jazz combo to play at resorts along the shore. His big-band hits include "One O'clock Jump" and "One Two Three Alairy."

Frank Sinatra developed his singing style at the Rustic Cabin, a roadhouse in his hometown of Hoboken. By 1942, crowds of screaming teenaged girls trailed him wherever he went. His fans adorned his house with lipstick messages: "Frankie Darling," and "Frankie, I love you!" Sinatra's popularity as a "crooner" vaulted him to a successful career in Hollywood. His film appearances include *From Here to Eternity, Guys and Dolls*, and *The Man with the Golden Arm*. Sinatra continued to produce top-selling records for nearly five decades.

In the mid 1970s, New Jersey saw the rise of a new teenage idol, a singer-songwriter from Freehold named Bruce Springsteen. Springsteen's first album, *Greetings from Asbury Park, New Jersey*, is

The New Jersey Symphony Orchestra performing at an outdoor July 4 concert

a salute to his early days of struggle and disappointment, when he performed in night spots along that town's boardwalk. Springsteen's 1975 album, *Born to Run*, won him an international reputation. His music continues to celebrate the lives of ordinary working people. Many of his songs are inspired by his New Jersey roots.

While popular music plays a key role, New Jerseyans also have a deep appreciation of the classics. In 1922, a small orchestra of string players gave its first performance at the Montclair Art Museum before an audience of one hundred people. In the 1927-28 season, the Montclair Orchestra merged with a group from East Orange to form the New Jersey Symphony. Now based in Newark, the symphony has performed at New York's Lincoln Center and Carnegie Hall, and at the John F. Kennedy Center for the Performing Arts in Washington, D.C. In 1972, the American Symphony Orchestra League listed the New Jersey Symphony as one of the nation's major orchestras.

SPORTS

On June 19, 1846, a curious crowd gathered around an empty lot in Hoboken as two nine-man teams, the Knickerbockers and the New Yorks, took their positions. Perhaps none of the spectators guessed that this strangely complicated game would someday become America's favorite pastime. They were witnessing the world's first game of organized baseball. The bat could be any length, the pitcher threw underhanded, and there were no strikes or balls. After four innings, the New Yorks beat the Knickerbockers 23-1. According to those early rules, the first team to score twenty-one points was the winner.

New Jersey was also the scene of the first intercollegiate football game in history. It was played between those two ancient rivals, Rutgers and Princeton, in New Brunswick on November 6, 1869. Rutgers won with a score of 6-4. According to legend, a stodgy professor passed as the game was in full swing. Shaking his umbrella at the pushing, shouting boys he exclaimed, "You will come to no good Christian end!" Ironically, seven of the Rutgers players went on to become ordained ministers.

As the state has no major-league baseball team of its own, most New Jerseyans follow the exploits of teams from New York or Philadelphia. Two major-league football teams, the Giants and the Jets, use the stadium at the Meadowlands Sports Complex as their home field. Yet, to the irritation of many New Jerseyans, both still refer to themselves as New York teams. For a short time, during the brief tenure of the United States Football League (USFL), New Jersey had a football team of its own, the New Jersey Generals.

The Brendan Byrne Arena at the Meadowlands is home to a pro basketball team, the New Jersey Nets, and to the ice-hockey team called the New Jersey Devils. The Cosmos soccer team, also based in the Meadowlands complex, won international renown in the late 1970s and early 1980s. The Cosmos' star player was the world-famous Brazilian soccer champion Pelé. Pelé lent the team his support in an attempt to win soccer a wider audience in the United States. Sadly, the Cosmos disbanded in 1985.

Most New Jersey football fans follow the Giants (above) or the Jets, both of whom play at Giants Stadium in the Meadowlands.

OUTDOOR RECREATION

The New Jersey seashore is a haven for millions of visitors each summer. For the adventurous, there are surfing and sailing, while those who wish to relax can build sand castles, wander along the boardwalk, or simply bask in the sun. Deep-sea fishermen catch bluefish, porgies, and mackerel. Digging for clams or crabbing with baited metal cages can be fun for the whole family.

The people of New Jersey have taken strong measures to preserve the state's woodlands and marshes. Forty state parks and eleven state forests provide opportunities for picnicking, hiking, boating, and bird-watching. While developers were planning the Meadowlands Sports Complex, environmentalists were fighting to save a substantial portion of the marshland as a wildlife sanctuary. Today mallard ducks, pheasants, and egrets nest in the shadow of Giants Stadium. One hundred thousand acres (40,470 hectares) of the Pinelands, that mysterious wilderness of marshes and pygmy forests, are protected as a unique habitat for wild orchids and other rare plants and animals.

Chapter 10

A BRIEF TOUR OF NEW JERSEY

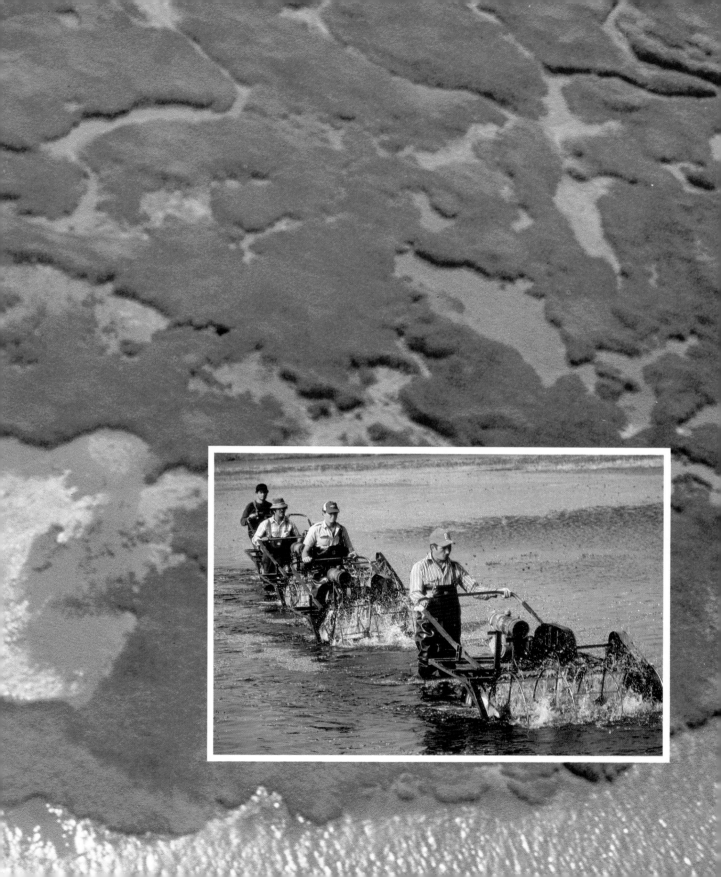

A BRIEF TOUR OF NEW JERSEY

From the industrial cities of the Hudson waterfront to the Pinelands of the south, a trip through New Jersey is a journey of discovery. A traveler passing from region to region, even from one county to the next, is struck by the dramatic contrasts in landscape and life-style.

THE NORTHEASTERN CITIES

For good or ill, the development of northeastern New Jersey has been shaped from the beginning by the region's proximity to New York. As early as the nineteenth century, New York provided an ever-hungry market for farm produce from present-day Bergen County, for Paterson's silks, and for Newark's fine leather shoes. By the time of the Civil War, New Yorkers realized that New Jersey was not only a producer of goods but a fine place to live. In search of the peaceful country life, they bought up parcels of land west of the Hudson and commuted by ferry each day to their jobs in Manhattan. Today, automobiles clog a sprawling maze of highways during morning and evening rush hours, as the modern descendants of those early commuters battle back and forth from homes in the New Jersey suburbs to New York offices and factories. Many view this part of New Jersey as little more than New York City's bedroom.

Yet, not all the people of this region are commuters. Thousands of men and women work in the factories and chemical plants of

Port Newark
is located in
New Jersey's
largest city.

Newark, Elizabeth, Rahway, and Passaic. And although the New
York skyline towers on the horizon, the towns and cities of
northeastern New Jersey cling stubbornly to a character all their
own.

First settled in 1666, Newark is the largest city in New Jersey.
Newark's leather industry was well established by 1810. In 1818,
Seth Boyden, who moved to Newark from New England,
manufactured the first patent leather ever produced in the United
States. Seagoing ships, including whalers, sailed into Newark
Harbor. Early on, Newark acquired a reputation as a bustling,
boisterous big city. In 1822, one indignant Newark woman
complained that the streets "are overrun with ignorance and
profanity; and often the Sabbath is made a season of all most
ungovernable noise and confusion."

Today, much of Newark's inner city is blighted by poverty. But
the city still has much to be proud of. The Newark Museum
displays natural history exhibits and an excellent art collection. It

also houses an unusual collection of antique fire engines and fire-fighting equipment. Newark's colleges include the New Jersey Institute of Technology and a branch of Rutgers University. Lovely Branchbrook Park boasts more varieties of flowering cherry trees than Washington, D.C. Newark also is home to busy Newark International Airport, though part of the site is within the Elizabeth city limits.

Another interesting city in northeastern New Jersey is culturally minded Montclair, with its art museum, little theaters, and rows of elegant Victorian mansions. Hudson River waterfront cities such as Hoboken, Jersey City, and Bayonne still have their share of heavy industry. But their image is changing as young professionals restore decaying nineteenth-century homes. Other communities, such as Cedar Grove, Little Falls, and the Caldwells, are primarily residential. With their shaded streets and manicured lawns, they are the peaceful refuge at the end of the traffic jam after a long day's work.

THE NORTHWESTERN MOUNTAINS

As one heads west, leaving New York behind, patches of woodland break up the landscape of cities and towns. Here and there a crystal lake glistens among the hills. Closer to the Delaware River, the hills become low mountains, offering some of the most breathtaking scenery to be found in the state.

Too rocky for intensive vegetable farming, Sussex, Warren, Hunterdon, and other counties of northwestern New Jersey proved ideal for dairying and poultry raising. Mining was also a key industry in the region well into the twentieth century. The state's first copper mine, at Pahaquarry in Sussex County, began to operate in 1657. Ironworks opened at Hanover in 1710, and by

Although in many areas New Jersey land was too rocky for full-scale vegetable farming, many counties proved ideal for dairy farming.

the time of the revolutionary war, the Morristown area led the colonies in iron mining and smelting. After the Civil War, Franklin became the nation's top producer of zinc, a position it held for nearly a century.

Until the late 1960s, northwestern New Jersey remained largely rural. Then, in the 1970s and 1980s, corporations and real-estate developers discovered the potential of so much open space within an easy drive of New York. Today, woods and small farms are making way for condominiums and industrial research centers. Fortunately, however, some developers have taken pains to preserve the area's natural beauty. Gleaming new housing complexes are interlaced with tracts of forest, and would-be gardeners sometimes grumble that the wild deer get more than their fair share of the tomatoes and zucchini.

Morristown is among the most fascinating cities in this region

The Morris County Park Commission has offices in this beautiful nineteenth-century mansion on the grounds of the Frelinghuysen Arboretum in Morristown.

of New Jersey. Magnificent prerevolutionary mansions are vivid reminders of the British gentry who brought their Old-World style to the colonies. Through the nineteenth century, while cities farther east clattered with industry, Morristown remained comfortable, quiet, and self-contained. The town never lost its aura of affluence. In 1900, more millionaires lived in Morristown than in any other city of comparable size in the world.

In 1929, Morristown was chosen as headquarters for The Seeing Eye, the first school in America to train guide dogs. Blind men and women train at the Seeing Eye for four weeks, developing the necessary rapport with their dogs before they return home. Dog and human learn to work as an effective team on downtown Morristown's busy streets.

THE LOWER DELAWARE

Describing its position between New York City and Philadelphia, a writer once called New Jersey "a valley of humility between two mountains of conceit." Much as New York affected the development of northeastern New Jersey, the region along the lower Delaware was molded by Philadelphia. Since colonial days, Philadelphia has been a ready market for southern New Jersey's farm produce. Later, manufactured goods were sold there as well. Commuters once steamed back and forth by ferry across the Delaware from South Jersey to their jobs in Philadelphia. Today, bridges span the river, and most commuters travel to and from work by car.

Philadelphia's impact on southwestern New Jersey is undeniable. Yet this region is, in a sense, New Jersey's heartland. As one travels south, the wooded mountains of the north disappear. With its rich, loamy soil, the flat, open land of South Jersey is some of the most productive farmland in the nation. While the cities along the Delaware are major industrial centers, this is still essentially a rural region dotted with farms and small towns. It is home to New Jersey's two most famous universities, Rutgers and Princeton, and to Trenton, the state capital.

When Trenton was selected as New Jersey's capital in 1790, the town consisted of a few muddy streets, a public pump, and a whipping post. Today the city's motto proclaims, "Trenton makes—the world takes." Trenton is a leading producer of electrical equipment, processed rubber, and metal products. It is also the home of the Lenox China Company, known throughout the world for its fine dinnerware. Ever since Woodrow Wilson ordered seventeen hundred pieces in 1918, Lenox has been the official White House china.

Princeton
★ Trenton
Philadelphia
Camden
Salem
Bivalve
Port Norris

The golden dome of the state capitol in Trenton

The golden dome of the state capitol rises above downtown Trenton. Not far from the capitol stands the complex of buildings known as the New Jersey Cultural Center, consisting of the state library, a planetarium, and the state museum. The museum features historical exhibits and an excellent art collection. Visitors can also admire the 150-foot (46-meter) monument that commemorates the Battle of Trenton. On Christmas night, 1776, George Washington crossed the Delaware, defeated the Hessians, and revived the flagging spirits of the Continental army.

In 1890, a writer described the city of Camden as "crystallizing the life of southern New Jersey and offering a thousand streams of influence and succor to its giant companion on the west side of the Delaware." Commuters ferried back and forth between Camden and Philadelphia long before the Civil War. But around the turn of the century, Camden developed important industries of its own. In 1897, the Campbell's Canning Company, using locally produced meats and vegetables, introduced condensed soups to the American public. Originally one 10-ounce (284-gram) can of Campbell's Soup sold for ten cents. Shipyards opened in 1900, and Camden built many of the naval vessels that served in World War II. In 1901, the Victor Talking Machine Company, betting on an invention Thomas Edison described as a mere toy, began to manufacture phonographs and records.

Today Camden's shipyards are closed. The city has been losing industry and people since 1950. During the 1970s, the city's population fell by 17 percent. While statewide unemployment in 1985 stood at 4.4 percent, 12.6 percent of the people of Camden were without jobs. In 1915, city officials called Camden "the biggest little city in the world." Today, Camden is fighting for its very survival.

One symbol of survival in the western lowlands is the huge oak tree that stands in Salem's old Quaker cemetery. One humorist quipped that the tree, whose upper branches spread some 135 feet (41 meters), is "four years older than the Atlantic Ocean." Scientists calculate that the tree is actually between four and five hundred years old. It is believed to have been the site of a 1675 treaty between the Quakers and the Lenape Indians. Certainly it has looked on astonishing changes through the centuries. Camden's old oyster-shell roads have been replaced by asphalt,

Oystermen in Delaware Bay, where oysters are once again becoming big business

and Salem County now has canning factories, chemical plants, and a nuclear generating station. Through the ebb and flow of human concerns, the ancient Salem oak lives on, unmoved.

Until the 1950s, oysters were big business in Bivalve, Port Norris, and other towns along Delaware Bay. Then a strange parasite attacked the oyster beds, and each year the harvest declined. But in 1985, the oyster population showed the first signs of recovery. Perhaps the oystermen's way of life, wedded to wind and tide, may still endure.

THE PINELANDS AND THE SHORE

As one travels inland away from the Delaware River, the towns become smaller and more widely scattered. Cultivated land gives way to marshes and dense, low forests of pine and white cedar. This is the unique region known as the Pine Barrens, or Pinelands. Covering 1.3 million acres (526,109 hectares) and stretching

Cranberries grown in the bogs of the Pinelands are among New Jersey's leading crops.

nearly 80 miles (129 kilometers) from Cape May to the southern edge of Monmouth County, the Pinelands is the largest tract of undeveloped land between Boston and Washington, D.C.

Convinced that the wet, sandy soil was useless for agriculture, early white settlers called the area the Pine Barrens. But wild cranberries and blueberries flourished in the marshes, or bogs. In the 1880s, a few enterprising farmers experimented with the cultivation of these wild bushes. Today, cranberries and blueberries rank among New Jersey's leading crops.

The people of the Pinelands are thought to descend from Tory refugees and Hessian deserters of the revolutionary war. In later years, they may have been joined by men and women who sought to escape the pressures of civilization. Over the years they christened the villages, hills, and streams of the Pinelands with some of the most picturesque names to be found on any map: Apple Pie Hill, Bread and Cheese Run, Mount Misery, and Ong's Hat.

In 1916, a social worker named Elizabeth Kite published the first report about the appalling living conditions in the Pinelands. Medical facilities did not exist, children rarely attended school,

103

and hunger was sometimes rampant. State and federal programs have opened schools and clinics and cut roads to the most isolated villages. Today, many Pineland inhabitants work in the cranberry bogs or join highway-construction crews. Some act as guides in the state forests. Since Mrs. Kite's report, the people of the Pinelands have slowly but steadily moved toward America's mainstream.

In sharp contrast to the brooding quiet of the Pinelands is the teeming activity of New Jersey's shore resorts at the height of the summer season. New Jersey's beaches extend for 127 miles (204 kilometers), from Cape May north to Sandy Hook. To millions of vacationers each year, the Jersey shore is a paradise of shining sand, crashing breakers, wheeling gulls, and cool ocean breezes.

The town of Cape May, at New Jersey's southernmost tip, has been a resort throughout its history. After the Civil War, railroad tycoons and wealthy industrialists built vacation homes in Cape May, using what they believed to be classic European designs. The result is a bewildering architectural hodgepodge. An ornate Victorian mansion stands beside a Swiss chalet; a Tudor castle glares at an Italian villa across the street. Ludicrous as these combinations may be, they all add to the charm of old Cape May.

In 1976, the fading seaside town of Atlantic City on Absecon Island legalized casino gambling. Almost overnight, it became America's most popular ocean resort. In 1695, a Quaker named Thomas Budd bought 400 acres (162 hectares) of land on Absecon Island for four cents an acre (.4 hectares). In 1982, a single acre (.4 hectares) of prime boardwalk property sold for two million dollars. More than a dozen casino-hotels now line Atlantic City's boardwalk, luring millions of visitors each year with the dream of sudden riches.

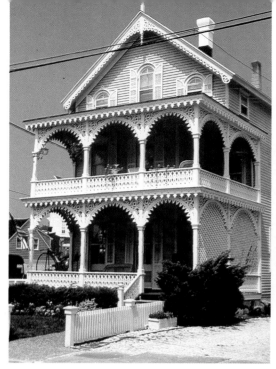

The resort towns of Cape May, with its interesting vacation homes (left), and Seaside Park, with its typical New Jersey boardwalk (above), teem with activity at the height of the summer season.

Atlantic City has many lesser-known attractions as well. The Brigantine National Wildlife Refuge, a few miles north of Absecon Island, is alive with nesting herons, ducks, terns, and gulls. And there is Lucy, the 65-foot- (20-meter-) high wooden elephant. Visitors climb a spiral staircase in Lucy's left hind leg to view the coast from a platform on her immense back.

The Atlantic City boardwalk was the brainchild of Alex Boardman, a Camden Atlantic Railroad conductor who knew the hotels were tired of sweeping up the sand that vacationers tracked into the hotels. On Sunday, June 26, 1870, the city opened a shaky, 1-mile- (1.6-kilometer-) long plank footpath that rested on pillars above the beach. Today, Atlantic City's boardwalk stretches for nearly 7 miles (11 kilometers).

The idea spread quickly. By the turn of the century, the boardwalk was a fixture at nearly every resort along the shore. The boardwalks offer something for every mood and occasion. In places, they are raucous with the cries of vendors. There are

Sandy Hook Lighthouse, which began operating in 1764, is the oldest continuously operating lighthouse in the country.

also quiet stretches where one can stroll along chewing saltwater taffy and breathing in the tangy salt air.

Heading north along the coast, travelers pass through one resort town after another: Seabright, Sea Isle City, Allenhurst, Asbury Park. The town of Long Branch in Monmouth County has an especially fascinating history.

Shortly after the Civil War, a group of wealthy businessmen decided to create a new tradition in this peaceful resort community. In the summer of 1869, they invited President Ulysses S. Grant to Long Branch, promising a quiet retreat from the heat and bustle of Washington. Grant fell in love with the town and returned to this "summer capital" year after year.

The businessmen's scheme worked on a grand scale. For the next thirty years, Long Branch was a summer playground for presidents—and for dozens of the rich and the powerful who traveled (or wished to travel) in their circle.

Rutherford B. Hayes visited regularly. After being critically wounded by an assassin, President James Garfield insisted on being taken to Long Branch, where he died in September 1881. Benjamin Harrison and William McKinley both were frequent visitors.

Gone was the tranquility that once had lured President Grant. High-rollers and gamblers trailed after the presidential elite. Elegant gaming clubs abounded, sporting gaudy chandeliers and marble-topped roulette tables. Diamond Jim Brady rode up and down Ocean Avenue with a fleet of electric cars, and Jubilee Jim Fisk hove into port at the helm of a 345-foot (105-meter) steamer that had his face painted on the boiler. Finally, in the 1890s, zealous reformers closed down the gambling houses. The glamorous days of the summer capital faded into memories, and Long Branch once more became a quiet family resort.

From the northeastern corner of Monmouth County a long, curving finger of sand reaches into Newark Bay. This is Sandy Hook, where Giovanni da Verrazano anchored his ship in 1524. Verrazano was the first European ever to sight the New Jersey coast. Perhaps Sandy Hook, this landmark in the state's earliest recorded history, is a fitting place to close this short tour of New Jersey.

On June 11, 1764, the Sandy Hook Lighthouse sent forth its first beams to guide ships safely on their way. The Sandy Hook Lighthouse is the oldest continuously operating lighthouse in the United States. It still gleams for passing ships today, a beacon of welcome from the shores of New Jersey.

New Jersey has often been overshadowed by its larger neighbors, and some argue that the state needs to develop a new image. But with its contributions to every era in American history, New Jersey already has a positive image. At long last, the world is beginning to recognize New Jersey's remarkable achievements.

FACTS AT A GLANCE

GENERAL INFORMATION

Statehood: December 18, 1787, third state

Origin of Name: New Jersey was named for the Isle of Jersey in the English Channel.

State Capital: Trenton, founded 1790

State Nickname: The "Garden State"

State Flag: Adopted in 1896, New Jersey's flag shows the state seal against a gold background. Centered on the seal is a shield with three plows upon it, representing the state's agriculture. The Greek goddess Ceres stands to the right of the shield, holding a horn of plenty. Liberty stands to the left. A horse's head can be seen above a sovereign helmet. The state motto, "Liberty and Prosperity," appears on a banner. The banner bears the date 1776, the year when New Jersey signed the Declaration of Independence.

State Motto: "Liberty and Prosperity"

State Bird: Eastern goldfinch

State Animal: Horse

State Flower: Purple violet

State Tree: Red oak

State Song: None

POPULATION

Population: 7,364,823, ninth among the states (1980 census)

Population Density: 940 people per sq. mi. (363 people per km²)

Population Distribution: 89 percent urban, 11 percent rural

A crowded urban
neighborhood
in Jersey City

Major Urban Centers:

Newark 329,248
Jersey City 223,532
Paterson... 137,970
Elizabeth 106,201
Trenton 92,124
Camden 84,910
East Orange... 77,025
Clifton 74,388
Bayonne... 65,047
Irvington 61,493
Union City.. 55,593
Vineland 53,753

(Population figures according to 1980 census)

Population Growth: New Jersey has experienced steady growth throughout its history. The greatest growth spurt occurred between 1900 and 1940, when the population more than doubled. In recent years, however, its growth has tapered off compared to that of the country as a whole. Between 1970 and 1980, New Jersey's population grew 2.7 percent, in contrast with the national rate of 11.4 percent. The table below shows population growth in New Jersey since 1790.

Year	Population
1790	184,139
1820	277,575
1840	373,306
1860	672,035
1880	1,131,116
1900	1,883,669
1920	3,155,900
1940	4,160,165
1950	4,835,329
1960	6,066,782
1970	7,171,112
1980	7,364,823

GEOGRAPHY

Borders: Save for a 38-mi. (61-km) stretch of inland border with New York State, New Jersey is entirely surrounded by water. To the north, the Hudson River comprises most of the border with New York. The Delaware River divides New Jersey from Pennsylvania and Delaware to the west. Delaware Bay forms the southern border. The Atlantic Ocean lies to the east.

Highest Point: High Point, in the Kittatinny Mountains, 1,803 ft. (550 m)

Lowest Point: Sea level, along the Atlantic coast

Greatest Distances: North to south—166 mi. (267 km)
East to west—57 mi. (92 km)

Area: 7,836 sq. mi. (20,295 km²)

Rank in Area Among the States: Forty-sixth

Coastline: 127 mi. (204 km) from Cape May to Sandy Hook

Bays: New Jersey's coastline is cut with a series of bays and inlets. Traveling from south to north, the bays include Great Egg Harbor, Little Egg Harbor, Barnegat, Sandy Hook, Raritan, and Newark.

Rivers: New Jersey's longest rivers are the Hudson and the Delaware, which comprise its borders with New York to the north and Pennsylvania and Delaware to the west. The longest river lying wholly within the state is the Raritan, which flows 75 mi. (121 km) from Morris County in the northwest to Raritan Bay. Other important rivers in the northern part of the state are the Passaic, the Hackensack, and the Musconetcong. Rivers in the south include the Maurice, Mullica, Great Egg Harbor, and Toms.

Lakes: New Jersey has some eight hundred natural and man-made lakes and ponds. Most are found in the northern part of the state. Greenwood Lake lies partly in New York. Lake Hopatcong is the largest lake lying entirely within the state. Other lakes include Budd, Sunfish, Green Pond, Culver, Swartswood, and Lake Mohawk.

Topography: The movement of the Wisconsin Glacier carved northern New Jersey into a series of low mountain ranges, while the southern part of the state remained predominantly flat. Geologists divide New Jersey into four main topographical regions: The Appalachian Ridge and Valley; the New England Highlands; the Piedmont Plateau; and the Atlantic Coastal Plain.
The Appalachian Ridge and Valley region, in the northwest corner of the state, is a portion of the Appalachian Ridge, which runs from New York to Alabama. It comprises about one-tenth of the state's area, and includes the Kittatinny Mountains. The New England Highlands region also comprises about one-tenth of

the state's area. It consists of low, flat-topped mountains about 1,000 ft. (305 m) in height. The Piedmont Plateau, comprising about one-fifth of the state's area, covers the northeastern section of the state. It includes the Ramapo and Watchung mountains, about 900 ft. (274 m), and the Palisades along the Hudson River. The Atlantic Coastal Plain, a region untouched by the great glacier, comprises about three-fifths of the state—all of the land south of Trenton and Perth Amboy. This region is generally flat, rising to about 400 ft. (122 m) at its highest elevation. This portion of New Jersey is part of the plain that runs along the Atlantic coast from Cape Cod to Florida.

Climate: New Jersey's climate is relatively mild for a northern state. Southern New Jersey, especially near the coast, tends to be somewhat warmer than the northern part of the state. In July, the temperature averages 70° F. (21° C) in the north and 76° F. (24° C) in the south. Average temperatures in January are 36° F. (2.2° C) in the north and 34° F. (1.1° C) in the south. The highest temperature ever recorded was 110° F. (43° C), on July 10, 1936, at Runyon. The lowest recorded temperature was -34° F. (-36.7° C), on January 5, 1904, at River Vale.

NATURE

Trees: The forests of northern New Jersey are composed mainly of hardwood trees, including oak, maple, dogwood, beech, and ash. Evergreens are more common in the south. In southern New Jersey's Pinelands, the forests contain white cedar, pine, and oak trees.

Flowers: A wide variety of wildflowers grow all over New Jersey. These include violets, Queen Anne's lace, lady's slippers, buttercups, and daisies. Rare wild orchids bloom in the Pinelands.

Animals: Many wild animals survive even in urbanized areas. These include rabbits, squirrels, chipmunks, raccoons, opossums, skunks, and even deer. Foxes, otters, muskrats, and some eastern bobcats can be found in rural regions. Whales are occasionally glimpsed offshore, and bottlenosed dolphins calve each spring in Delaware Bay. The Pinelands is the only known habitat of the mouselike bog lemming.

Birds: Many bird species nest in New Jersey, and hundreds more pass through the state during spring and fall migrations. Familiar songbirds include the robin, mourning dove, house finch, cardinal, catbird, and mockingbird. Many species of gulls, terns, ducks, and herons nest in New Jersey's marshlands. Birdwatchers gather every spring to spot migrating hawks and eagles at Cape May.

Fish: Sport fishermen on New Jersey's lakes catch sunfish, perch, catfish, pickerel, large-mouth bass, and rainbow trout. Ocean game fish include striped bass, porgies, bluefish, fluke, and flounder.

New Jersey is blessed with many beautiful natural areas and an abundance of wildlife. Left: The Great Gorge, Vernon Valley. Right: A wood duck.

GOVERNMENT

The state government of New Jersey, like the federal government, has three branches—legislative, judicial, and executive.

The legislative branch, or state legislature, consists of an upper house, or senate, and a lower house, or assembly. It votes on new laws and determines how state revenues will be spent.

The judicial branch consists of an extensive court system, including municipal and county courts, superior courts, and the state supreme court in Trenton. Cases may be appealed from a lower court to a higher one when questions arise about the interpretation of the law.

The governor executes, or carries out, the law. The governor of New Jersey is elected for four years and may hold two consecutive terms. Article V, Section II of the state constitution says, "The Governor may grant pardons and reprieves in all cases other than impeachment and treason." The governor appoints most executive officials, and is commander-in-chief of the state militia.

Number of Counties: 21

U.S. Representatives: 14

Electoral Votes: 16

EDUCATION

New Jersey spends an average of $4,007 per year to educate each student in the public schools. This is the fourth-highest per-student expenditure in the nation.

New Jersey has 1,788 elementary schools and 405 secondary schools. A total of 1,147,571 children attend the state's public schools. New Jersey has one teacher for every 15.6 students.

New Jersey's outstanding preparatory schools include Blair Academy at Blairstown, Montclair Academy in Montclair, and the Lawrenceville School in Lawrenceville near Princeton.

New Jersey has thirty-two accredited institutions of higher learning. Rutgers University, with branches in New Brunswick, Newark, and Camden, is the official state university. The state colleges are Montclair, William Paterson in Wayne Township, Jersey City, Trenton, Glassboro, Ramapo in Mahwah, Stockton, and Kean College of New Jersey in Union. Among the privately controlled schools are Princeton University and Westminster Choir College in Princeton, Fairleigh Dickinson University at Rutherford, Drew University in Madison, Rider College in Lawrenceville, and the Stevens Institute of Technology in Hoboken.

ECONOMY AND INDUSTRY

Principal Products
Agriculture: New Jersey's agricultural products have an estimated annual value of $409 million. They include tomatoes, cabbage, lettuce, cucumbers, squash, melons, pumpkins, corn, potatoes, blueberries, cranberries, peaches, apples, poultry, eggs, and dairy products.

Manufacturing: New Jersey's manufactured goods are valued at approximately $24.7 billion per year. They include pharmaceuticals, cosmetics, plastics, processed foods, electrical equipment, nonelectrical machinery, glass, processed rubber, and paper products.

Natural Resources: Minerals mined in New Jersey are valued at $152 million a year. They include iron ore, basalt (used in road construction), limestone, granite, clay, and green sand marl (used in fertilizers and water softeners).

Fishing: New Jersey's fishing industry is valued at $53 million per year. The state produces about 40 percent of the clams consumed nationwide. Fish caught commercially off New Jersey include flounder, menhaden, porgy, sea bass, tilefish, and whiting.

Business: Of the leading one hundred corporations in the nation, eighty-five have some operations in New Jersey. The state's largest corporation is AT&T. Other corporations based in New Jersey include Bell Labs, Standard Oil of New Jersey, Prudential Insurance, Mutual Benefit Life Insurance, Hoffmann LaRoche, Johnson and Johnson, American Cyanamid, and Campbell's Soup.

Tourism brings approximately $8.5 billion to New Jersey each year. Tourists are attracted to New Jersey's many seaside resorts, ski resorts, state parks, restored villages, the Meadowlands complex, and the gambling casinos at Atlantic City.

Port Newark is one of the busiest cargo ports in the world.

Communication: New Jersey has 255 newspapers, 30 of them dailies. The state's largest paper is the *Newark Star-Ledger*. Other leading newspapers include the *Bergen Record* of Hackensack, the *Asbury Park Press*, the *Camden Courier-Post* and the *Trenton Times*. New Jersey has approximately 90 commercial radio stations. WJZ of Newark, which began operating in 1921, was the second commercially licensed radio station in the country. The oldest continuously operating radio station in New Jersey is WTNJ, formerly called WAAT, which began broadcasting in 1923. New Jersey's only VHF (very high frequency) television station, WOR, broadcasts from Secaucus. Eight UHF (ultrahigh frequency) television stations operate within the state. Publishers in New Jersey include Prentice-Hall in Englewood Cliffs, Silver, Burdett & Ginn, Inc. in Morristown, Troll Books in Mahwah, Princeton University Press in Princeton, and Rutgers University Press in New Brunswick.

Transportation: New Jersey has 265 airports. By far the largest is Newark International Airport. Covering 2,300 acres (931 hectares), Newark Airport served more than 29 million passengers in 1985.

The Port of Newark, controlled by the Port Authority of New York and New Jersey, is New Jersey's only major cargo port. It is one of the busiest ports in the world.

New Jersey's two main highways are the New Jersey Turnpike and the Garden State Parkway. Altogether, New Jersey has 33,100 mi. (53,258 km) of highways and roads.

About 100 towns and cities in New Jersey can be reached by train. The state has 1,650 mi. (2,655 km) of railroad tracks. Port Authority Trans Hudson (PATH) trains that run between New Jersey and New York City are used by tens of thousands of commuters.

The Delaware Water Gap is a deep, scenic valley carved
by the Delaware River through the Kittatinny Mountains.

SOCIAL AND CULTURAL LIFE

Museums: The Newark Museum is the largest museum in New Jersey. It has fine natural-history exhibits and an excellent art collection. Also displayed on the museum grounds are an authentic one-room schoolhouse and a collection of vintage fire engines and fire-fighting equipment. The Montclair Art Museum is noted for its collection of works by nineteenth-century painter George Inness, who lived in Montclair for many years. The New Jersey State Museum in Trenton displays paintings and sculpture, and has many fascinating natural-history exhibits. The four-story New Jersey Historical Society in Newark houses a sixty-thousand-volume library of books and periodicals relating to the state's history. The society's museum displays rotating exhibits on many New Jersey themes, and houses the world's greatest collection of objects and artifacts relating to New Jersey. The Ocean City Historical Museum recreates the story of Ocean City, an island resort off Cape May, in maps, pictures, and artifacts. A feature of special interest is the "Sindia Room," which displays relics salvaged from the *Sindia*, a sailing ship that went down offshore in 1901. The Van Riper House is a Dutch Colonial home that became the Wayne Township Historical Society in 1964. The home displays tools and furnishings typical of the period before the revolutionary war. The American Labor Museum, located in Haledon, depicts the way of life of immigrant workers during the late 1800s and early 1900s, and commemorates the 1913 Paterson silk-mill strike with photographs and artifacts.

Libraries: The first library in New Jersey was founded by Thomas Cadwalader in Trenton in 1750. Today, the state has 380 public libraries. Princeton University, with more than 3 million volumes, has the largest library in the state.

Music: While the people of New Jersey have access to the excellent symphonies of New York and Philadelphia, New Jersey has many fine orchestras of its own. Based in Newark, the New Jersey Symphony has performed at New York's Carnegie Hall and the John F. Kennedy Center in Washington. In 1972, the American Symphony Orchestra League listed the New Jersey Symphony as one of the nation's leading orchestras. Among New Jersey's semiprofessional orchestras are the Livingston Symphony, the Haddonfield Symphony, and the Masterwork Chamber Orchestra and Chorus of Morristown.

The Garden State Arts Center in Holmdel, with its open-sided amphitheater and surrounding lawn, presents classical and popular music, opera, ballet, and other types of professional entertainment throughout the summer. Princeton University's McCarter Treater has a resident theater company and also hosts Broadway companies on tour and other events.

Sports and Recreation: New Jersey's professional sports teams play at the Meadowlands Sports Complex in East Rutherford. New Jersey teams include the National Basketball Association (NBA) Nets and the National Hockey League (NHL) New Jersey Devils. Though two National Football League (NFL) teams, the Giants and the Jets, play in the Meadowlands stadium, they are considered New York teams. The Cosmos soccer team also played at the Meadowlands until it disbanded in 1985, as did the United States Football League (USFL) New Jersey Generals, until that league was dissolved in 1986.

New Jersey has forty state parks and eleven state forests. The woods, marshes, and seashore of the state's parklands serve as natural habitats for wildlife and recreation areas for people. Jersey City's Liberty State Park, near the Statue of Liberty and Ellis Island, was opened in 1977. Reclaimed from an industrial wasteland along the banks of the Hudson River, the park offers an excellent view of the Manhattan skyline. Hawks, eagles, and dolphins can be observed from the state park at Cape May Point. At the Hackensack Meadowlands Environmental Center, nature lovers may watch ducks, pheasants, and herons within a few hundred yards of the sprawling sports complex. Palisades Interstate Park, at the basalt cliffs on the west bank of the lower Hudson River, offers beautiful views of the Hudson. The deep, scenic valley carved by the Delaware River through the Kittatinny Mountains is the heart of the Delaware Water Gap National Recreation Area, which lies partly in Pennsylvania.

Historic Sites and Landmarks:

Allaire Village, in Allaire State Park, Monmouth County, is a restored bog-iron-mining village. Among the buildings that are open to visitors are the blacksmith shop, carpenter shop, general store, and bakery.

Barnegat Lighthouse, called "Old Barney," stands in a state park on Long Beach Island at the entrance to Barnegat Inlet.

The iron master's house at the restored colonial village of Batsto

Batsto Village, in Wharton State Forest in southeastern New Jersey, is a restored colonial village. Visitors can tour the ironworks where cannonballs were made for George Washington's army. The village is complete with a post office, general store, and several restored homes.

Clark Thread Company, a 13-acre (5-hectare) historic district in East Newark, contains thirty-five buildings constructed between 1875 and 1910. The Clark Thread Company once led the nation in the manufacture of cotton sewing thread.

Craig House stands near the site of the 1778 Battle of Monmouth. On display at this colonial farmhouse are muskets and cannons from the revolutionary war era.

Edison National Historic Site in West Orange is the site where Thomas Edison set up his "invention factory" in 1887. Open to visitors are his office and library, and workshop with examples of many of his creations, including the phonograph, motion-picture camera, and electric light.

Fairview District in Camden was the site of a model community built for factory workers before World War I. Narrow circular streets surround a central square. The historic district contains nearly one thousand houses built in a variety of styles.

Morristown National Historical Park was created as a memorial to George Washington and the Continental army. Morristown was Washington's base of operations during two winters of the revolutionary war. The colonial Jacob Ford Mansion, now a museum, served as his headquarters during the bitter winter of 1779-1780, and at Jockey Hollow, outside the town, visitors can see reconstructions of the log huts used by the troops during that terrible winter.

Wallace House, in Somerville, was General Washington's headquarters from December 1778 to June 1779

Nassau Hall, a stone building at the heart of Princeton University's campus, was built in 1756. During the revolutionary war, it served as a barracks and hospital, first for the British and later for the Continental army. From June through November, 1783, Nassau Hall was the headquarters of the Continental Congress.

Old Dutch Parsonage in Somerville was the site of a seminary that eventually moved to New Brunswick and became Rutgers University.

Old Manse, located in Caldwell, is a nineteenth-century home that was the birthplace of President Grover Cleveland.

Paterson Historic District comprises 89 acres (36 hectares) of land surrounding the Great Falls of the Passaic River. This historic district preserves nineteenth-century locomotive works, a turn-of-the-century silk mill, and nearly forty other historic buildings.

Ringwood Manor, in Ringwood State Park, Passaic County, is a historic mansion built in 1810. Once the home of a succession of prominent iron-making families, it is surrounded by the remains of iron mines and forges dating back to 1740.

Wallace House, across the street from the Old Dutch Parsonage in Somerville, was General George Washington's headquarters from December 1778 to June 1779.

Walt Whitman House in Camden, built in 1848, became the poet's home in 1887. It is surrounded by a historical district in which several other Victorian houses are carefully preserved.

119

Weehawken Dueling Ground, on the Palisades overlooking the Hudson River, was the site of the 1804 duel between Aaron Burr and Alexander Hamilton.

Other Interesting Places to Visit:

Abbot Farm, in Hamilton Township, greater Trenton, was the site of some of the most important archaeological finds in New Jersey. Visitors can view ancient pottery and stone tools dating back to about 500 B.C.

Albert Einstein House at 112 Mercer Street in Princeton was Einstein's home from the early 1930s until his death in 1955.

Lambert Castle, in Paterson, was built in 1892 by Paterson silk magnate Catholina Lambert. The castle, modeled on Warwick Castle in England, contains personal documents and memorabilia of Garrett Hobart, vice-president under McKinley.

Morven, in Princeton, was built in the early 1750s by Richard Stockton, a signer of the Declaration of Independence. This mansion was the official residence of the state governor from 1957 to 1982.

Thomas Nast House in Morristown was the home of cartoonist Thomas Nast from 1871 to 1902. Now a private home, it is filled with Nast memorabilia, including early drawings of the donkey and elephant, which came to symbolize the Democratic and Republican parties.

Old Monroe Schoolhouse in Newton was built in 1819 of hand-carved stone. The one-room schoolhouse contains early primers and slates, and even a few willow switches.

Weehawken Dueling Ground, on the Palisades overlooking the Hudson River, is the site of the 1804 duel in which Aaron Burr shot and killed Alexander Hamilton. The area was used as a dueling ground until 1835, although dueling had been declared illegal.

Smithville, near Atlantic City, is a restored eighteenth-century town.

Zabriskie Red Mill, on the Saddle River in Paramus, was built in 1745. First used as a gristmill, it was converted to a textile mill during the Civil War, and manufactured army blankets for the Union soldiers.

IMPORTANT DATES

10,000 B.C.—The first Native American people, probably ancestors of the Lenape Indians, settle in the region now known as New Jersey

1524—Giovanni da Verrazano, sailing under the flag of France, anchors off Sandy Hook and explores the New Jersey shore around Newark Bay

1609—Henry Hudson, sailing for the Dutch East India Company, explores the New Jersey Shore, New York Harbor, and the Hudson River, and claims the entire region for The Netherlands

1614—Dutch fur trader Cornelius Jacobsen Mey explores Delaware Bay

1618—Dutch traders establish a trading post at Bergen, the first European settlement in New Jersey

1623—Cornelius Mey establishes Fort Nassau on the Delaware River just south of present-day Camden; when a Dutch ship returns eight years later, the colony has mysteriously disappeared

1633—The Dutch settle at Pavonia, near the site of present-day Jersey City

1643-1653—Swedes and Finns establish settlements along the lower Delaware River in today's Salem and Gloucester counties

1655—The Dutch gain control of the Finnish and Swedish settlements on the Delaware

1657—The Dutch open the first copper mine in New Jersey at Pahaquarry in present-day Sussex County

1664—King Charles II of England grants the Dutch lands in the New World to his brother James, Duke of York, and a British fleet takes possession of the territory without firing a shot; the area west of the Hudson becomes known as Nova Caesarea, or New Jersey

1665—The Duke of York gives New Jersey to two loyal supporters, John, Lord Berkeley, and Sir George Carteret

1666—Newark founded by settlers from Connecticut led by Robert Treat

1676—New Jersey is divided into East Jersey and West Jersey; East Jersey still belongs to Sir George Carteret, West Jersey bought by Quakers led by William Penn

1702—East and West Jersey united as a British crown colony, but share a governor with New York

Princeton University was founded in 1746.

1738—New Jersey gets its own governor, Lewis Morris, a wealthy landholder from Monmouth County

1739—Casper Wistar sets up glassworks in Salem County; Wistar glass later becomes a valuable collector's item

1746—A charter is granted to the College of New Jersey, later known as Princeton University

1758—Brotherton, the first Indian reservation in North America, founded at Indian Mills; it is a planned community for about two hundred of New Jersey's surviving Lenape people

1764—Sandy Hook Lighthouse, now the oldest continuously operating lighthouse in America, is built

1766—Queens College established, later renamed Rutgers University

1774—On the night of December 22, a band of townspeople in Greenwich dress as Indians and burn a cargo of British tea to protest import duties

1776—On June 21, New Jersey's Governor William Franklin, a British sympathizer, is arrested and sent to Connecticut; in August, William Livingston is elected New Jersey's first provincial governor; on Christmas night, General George Washington and his troops cross the Delaware and inflict a crushing defeat on the Hessian soldiers at Trenton in the most important battle in the early part of the revolutionary war

1777—Washington defeats the British at Princeton on January 3 and moves to winter quarters at Morristown

1778—Washington's army clashes with the British in the Battle of Monmouth on June 28; in this battle, the longest of the war, the Americans are defeated

1779-1780—Washington's army survives a grueling winter at Jockey Hollow near Morristown

1780—The British are defeated at the Battle of Springfield

1783—From June 28 to November 4, the Continental Congress meets at Princeton, which becomes the national capital during that period; there Congress receives news of the British surrender

1787—On December 18, New Jersey becomes the third state to ratify the United States Constitution

1790—Trenton established as the capital of New Jersey

1791—Alexander Hamilton's Society for Useful Manufactures (SUM) founds the city of Paterson on the Great Falls of the Passaic River; it is the first planned industrial city in the United States

1797—New Jersey extends voting rights to women and free blacks

1804—Aaron Burr kills Alexander Hamilton, a long-time political rival, in a duel at Weehawken; an act for the gradual abolition of slavery in New Jersey is passed— girls born into slavery are to be freed at age twenty-one, boys at age twenty-five

1807—After 279 percent of the eligible voters cast ballots in an election to decide the location of the Essex County Courthouse, women and blacks lose the right to vote; the measure is considered "highly necessary to the safety, quiet, good order, and dignity of the state"

1817—Princeton students rebelling against the strict discipline imposed by the college president lock up the entire faculty, set several buildings on fire, and hold Old North Hall for a day with pistols and cutlasses

1825—John Stevens operates the first railroad in America on a circular track in Hoboken

1830—Dr. Samuel Fowler perfects a process for making zinc-oxide powder, used as a paint base; the town of Franklin begins mining zinc and eventually becomes the world's leading zinc producer

1831—The Morris Canal is completed from Philipsburg to Newark; an ingenious system of locks enables barges to climb 913 ft. (278 m) from sea level to Lake Hopatcong, and then to descend 760 ft. (232 m) to Philipsburg; coal is shipped from Pennsylvania across New Jersey to Newark and from there on to New York

1834—The Delaware-Raritan Canal is completed, creating a link between Philadelphia and New York City

1838 — Samuel F.B. Morse and Alfred Vail transmit the world's first telegraph message in Morristown: "A patient waiter is no loser"; the Camden and Amboy Railroad is completed, crossing the state from Camden to Jersey City

1840 — Joseph Henry transmits the first radio signal at Princeton

1844 — A new state constitution is ratified; it gives the people of the state a bill of rights and extends the governor's term to three years

1846 — The world's first professional baseball game is played in Hoboken between the New York Baseball Club and the Knickerbocker Baseball Club

1860 — New Jersey gives Stephen A. Douglas the popular vote over Abraham Lincoln

1862 — Fort Delaware on Pea Patch Island becomes a prison for captured Confederate soldiers; some twelve thousand prisoners are crowded onto the tiny island, and twenty-five hundred die

1865 — The Civil War ends; altogether, New Jersey sent 88,306 men to the Union army

1869 — President Ulysses S. Grant spends the summer at Long Branch, the seaside resort that remains a presidential vacation spot for the next thirty years; Rutgers defeats Princeton in the world's first intercollegiate football game

1876 — Thomas Edison opens his first laboratory at Menlo Park

1877 — Edison makes first phonograph recording, "Mary Had a Little Lamb," at his Menlo Park laboratory

1879 — Edison develops the world's first practical incandescent light at Menlo Park; it burns for forty hours

1881 — President James A. Garfield, wounded by an assassin, comes to Elberon near Long Branch in the hope that the pure ocean air will bring about his recovery; he dies after two weeks

1884 — Grover Cleveland, born in Caldwell, is elected president of the United States; he is the only native-born New Jerseyan ever to become president

1893 — The world's first motion-picture studio, known as the "Black Maria," is completed at Edison's new laboratory in West Orange

1896 — Garrett A. Hobart of Paterson becomes vice-president of the United States under William McKinley

1907-1917 — Fort Lee is the capital of the motion-picture industry

1910—Woodrow Wilson, former president of Princeton University, is elected governor of New Jersey on a Progressive platform

1912—Woodrow Wilson is elected president of the United States

1913—A massive strike shuts down the silk mills of Paterson for five months

1917-1918—Powder plants in New Jersey produce more than half the American explosives used in World War I; shipyards in Camden, Newark, and other New Jersey cities produce battleships; planes are built in Plainfield, Elizabeth, and Keyport; Hoboken is the major port of embarkation for soldiers leaving from the east coast

1919—The first commercial airline carries passengers between Atlantic City and New York City

1921—WJZ, the world's second commercial radio station, begins broadcasting from Newark

1926—The Delaware River Bridge, now called the Benjamin Franklin Bridge, opens between Camden and Philadelphia

1927—The Holland Tunnel opens, linking Jersey City and New York

1929—Air service begins at Newark Airport

1931—George Washington Bridge opens between Fort Lee and Manhattan

1932—The world is shocked when the infant son of aviator Charles Lindbergh is kidnapped from the family's home near Hopewell; the child's body is later found in the nearby woods

1936—Bruno Richard Hauptmann, an unemployed carpenter, is executed in Trenton for the murder of the Lindbergh baby

1937—The German dirigible *Hindenburg* explodes and burns as it is about to land at Lakehurst, and thirty-six people die in the disaster; the Lincoln Tunnel opens between Weehawken and midtown Manhattan

1941-1945—New Jersey ranks fifth among the states in volume of war contracts; Curtiss-Wright Corporation in Paterson builds more airplane engines than any other airplane manufacturer; Fort Dix handles 1,300,000 draftees

1947—A new state constitution ratified by the state's voters allows the governor to hold two consecutive terms, increases state senators' terms from two to four years, and simplifies the court system

1951—The New Jersey Turnpike opens to traffic from the George Washington Bridge to Camden

1955—The Garden State Parkway is completed, running from Montville to Cape May

1962—Telstar, developed by Bell Labs, is launched into space; it is the world's first communications satellite

1966—New Jersey invokes its first sales tax

1967—A bloody street riot erupts in Newark's inner city; twenty-six people are killed, and the city suffers more than $10 million in property damage

1969—New Jersey approves a weekly state lottery

1976—The first legalized gambling casinos open in Atlantic City, and almost overnight, the once-decaying resort town becomes the nation's most popular vacation spot; the Meadowlands Sports Complex opens in East Rutherford

1981—New Jersey voters pass a $100-million bond issue to create a state fund for cleaning up hazardous wastes

1984—Congressman Frank Guarini brings to light documents that dispute New York's ownership of Ellis and Liberty islands; on New Jersey's behalf, he files a suit contending that the islands actually belong to New Jersey

1986—Ground is broken for what will be New Jersey's tallest office building, a thirty-story tower in Jersey City that will be 485 ft. (148 m) tall

1987—Richard Purdy Wilbur named poet laureate of the United States

1990—Governor James Florio signs the Clean Water Enforcement Act, which provides for stricter enforcement of the Water Pollution Control Act

IMPORTANT PEOPLE

EDWIN ALDRIN

William A. (Bud) Abbott (1896-1974), born in Asbury Park; comedian; best known for comedy routines performed with partner Lou Costello on stage, radio, television, and in movies

Edwin Eugene (Buzz) Aldrin (1930-   ), born in Cedarville; astronaut; served as copilot under Neil Armstrong on *Apollo XI* flight; on July 20, 1969, became the second man ever to set foot on the moon

William (Count) Basie (1904-1984), born in Red Bank; jazz pianist and composer; made his first big-band recording in 1937

Moe Berg (1902-1972), born in Newark; professional baseball player with the Brooklyn Dodgers, Chicago White Sox, and Boston Red Sox; scholar and linguist who studied off-season at the Sorbonne in Paris; as an American spy during World War II, posed as a German businessman and obtained vital information about Germany's efforts to build an atomic bomb

Lawrence Peter (Yogi) Berra (1925-   ), long-time resident of Montclair; professional baseball player and manager; named American League's Most Valuable Player of the Year in 1951, 1954, and 1955; beginning in 1947, served fourteen seasons as catcher with New York Yankees; won pennants as manager of both the Yankees and the Mets

Elias Boudinot (1740-1821), leader in the American Revolution; served as president of the Continental Congress (1782-83); practiced law in New Jersey for many years after the war; died in Burlington

Jim Bouton (1939-   ), born in Newark; professional baseball pitcher; his experiences as a pitcher with the New York Yankees furnished the background for his book, *Ball Four*, which revealed the behind-the-scenes lives of big-time baseball players of the 1960s and 1970s

William Warren (Bill) Bradley (1943-   ), college and professional basketball player, politician; earned an outstanding reputation on Princeton University's team; studied at Oxford University as a Rhodes Scholar; played professionally with the New York Knicks; retired from basketball in 1977; represented New Jersey as a United States senator (1978-   )

David Brearly (1745-1790), born in Spring Grove; obtained law degree from Princeton; in 1787 assisted in drafting the United States Constitution

Van Wyck Brooks (1886-1963), born in Plainfield; noted American literary critic; received the 1937 Pulitzer Prize in history for the first volume of his five-volume work, *Makers and Finders: A History of the Writer in America, 1800-1915*

Aaron Burr (1756-1836), born in Newark; statesman, adventurer; entered Princeton as a sophomore at age of thirteen; vice-president of the United States (1801-05); in 1804, killed his long-time political rival, Alexander Hamilton, in a duel at Weehawken that destroyed Burr's political career; later acquired 1 million acres (404,700 hectares) of land around New Orleans, where some believed he intended to establish his own empire; was accused of treason against the United States, but was acquitted

Clifford Philip Case (1904-1982), born in Franklin Park; politician; Republican senator from New Jersey (1954-78); in the Senate he supported legislation concerned with civil rights, education, health, and urban affairs

Grover Cleveland (1837-1908), born in Caldwell; twenty-second and twenty-fourth president of the United States; only native-born New Jerseyan ever to become president; only American president to be elected to two non-consecutive terms (1885-89 and 1893-97)

WILLIAM BRADLEY

VAN WYCK BROOKS

AARON BURR

GROVER CLEVELAND

LOU COSTELLO

MARY MAPES DODGE

THOMAS ALVA EDISON

ALBERT EINSTEIN

James Fenimore Cooper (1789-1851), born in Burlington; novelist; considered to be the first major novelist of the New World; best known for his Leatherstocking Tales, a series of romantic novels about frontier life that included *The Last of the Mohicans, The Deerslayer,* and *The Pathfinder*

Louis Francis (Lou) Costello (1908-1959), born in Paterson; comedian; best known for comedy routines performed with partner Bud Abbott on stage, radio, television, and in movies

Stephen Crane (1871-1900), born in Newark; novelist, short-story writer, poet; sometimes referred to as the father of the American psychological novel; best known for *The Red Badge of Courage,* his vivid novel about the Civil War

Mary Mapes Dodge (1831-1905), long-time resident of Newark; author of children's books; as a young widow with small children to support, she embarked on a literary career; edited children's magazine *St. Nicholas;* best known for children's classic, *Hans Brinker, or, The Silver Skates*

Asher Brown Durand (1796-1886), born in Jefferson Village, now known as Maplewood; foremost American engraver of the early nineteenth century

Thomas Alva Edison (1847-1931), considered by many to be the most gifted inventor the world has ever known; was almost entirely self-taught; in 1876 set up his first "invention factory" in Menlo Park; in 1887 moved to larger laboratory in West Orange; first invention was an electric vote recorder; most famous inventions include the phonograph, motion-picture camera, and the first affordable incandescent light

Albert Einstein (1879-1955), German-born physicist; immigrated to the United States in 1933; considered the greatest scientific genius of modern times; member of the Institute for Advanced Studies in Princeton from 1933 until his death; in 1921 received the Nobel Prize in physics for his work on the photoelectric effect; best known for his theory of relativity, which helped to explain the origin and structure of the universe

Millicent Fenwick (1910-   ), politician; served as a Republican congresswomen from New Jersey (1974-82); championed the causes of feminism, human rights, and honest government

Malcolm Forbes, Jr. (1947-   ), born in Morristown; publisher of *Forbes* magazine, a leading periodical on finance; attended Princeton University; one of the richest people in the United States; when once asked the secret to his financial success, replied, "Hard work, imagination, perseverance, and a father who left me a hundred million dollars"

Frederick Theodore Frelinghuysen (1817-1885), born in Millstone; lawyer, politician; served as secretary of state under President Chester A. Arthur (1881-85)

Philip Freneau (1752-1832), grew up in Mount Pleasant; poet known for his satirical verse; considered the first American poet of genuine merit

Kenneth Gibson (1932-   ), politician; mayor of Newark (1970-   ); one of the first blacks to become mayor of a major American city; worked to improve housing, health, education, and economic opportunity in Newark, a city devastated by riots in 1967

Allen Ginsburg (1926-   ), born in Newark; poet; leader among the "Beat Generation" of American poets that arose in the 1950s; most famous poem is *Howl*, published 1955

Frank Hague (1876-1956), born in Jersey City; politician; mayor of Jersey City (1917-47); built a powerful political machine based on bribery and other corrupt practices; during thirty-year reign as mayor, controlled Hudson County and much of entire state; was known as Frank "I Am the Law" Hague

William Frederick (Bull) Halsey (1882-1959), born in Elizabeth; naval officer; fleet admiral during World War II; commanded the South Pacific forces; his philosophy, "hit hard, hit fast, hit often," earned him his nickname

Alexander Hamilton (1752-1804), statesman; came to New Jersey in 1763; attended Elizabethtown Academy; served as the nation's first secretary of the treasury under George Washington; his dream of a great industrial city at the Great Falls of the Passaic River led to founding of Paterson in 1791; killed by long-time political rival Aaron Burr in a duel at Weehawken in 1804

George Inness (1825-1894), long-time resident of Montclair; painter; one of the greatest American landscape painters of the nineteenth century; the New Jersey countryside provided the subject for many of his paintings

Joyce Kilmer (1886-1918), born in New Brunswick; poet, literary critic; best remembered for poem "Trees"; killed in France during World War I

Dorothy Kirsten (1917-   ), born in Montclair; operatic soprano; in 1945 made her debut with the Metropolitan Opera as Mimi in *La Boheme*

William Livingston (1723-1790), long-time resident of Elizabethtown; lawyer, patriot, statesman; represented New Jersey at Continental Congress; signer of United States Constitution; first governor of New Jersey (1776-90)

F.T. FRELINGHUYSEN

ALLEN GINSBURG

WILLIAM HALSEY

DOROTHY KIRSTEN

ZEBULON PIKE

PAUL ROBESON

FRANK SINATRA

BRUCE SPRINGSTEEN

William Paterson (1745-1806), jurist; attorney general of New Jersey (1776-83); member of Constitutional Convention; signer of United States Constitution; United States senator (1789-90); governor of New Jersey (1790-93); associate justice of the United States Supreme Court (1793-1806)

Zebulon Montgomery Pike (1779-1813), born in Lamberton; army officer, explorer; famous for explorations of American West; in 1806 discovered spectacular mountain, Pike's Peak, which bears his name; as brigadier general in War of 1812, was killed in attack on York

Molly Pitcher (1754-1832), born in Trenton; heroine of revolutionary war; real name Mary Ludwig Hays McCauley; followed husband into Battle of Monmouth and carried pitchers of water to Continental army soldiers, thus earning her nickname; when husband collapsed from the heat, she is said to have taken his place and continued firing his cannon through rest of battle

Paul Bustill Robeson (1898-1976), born in Princeton; singer, actor; son of a former slave; attended Rutgers; All-American football player; obtained law degree from Columbia University; due to discrimination against blacks, was unable to establish law practice; turned to acting and singing; became disillusioned with America's treatment of blacks and looked to the Communist Party as an alternative; during McCarthy Era of early 1950s was blacklisted, and his career never recovered

Philip Roth (1933-   ), born in Newark; novelist; graduate of Rutgers; writes about Jewish life in America; his short novel *Good-bye, Columbus* won the National Book Award in 1960; other works include *Letting Go, Portnoy's Complaint,* and *The Professor of Desire*

Walter Marty Schirra, Jr. (1923-   ), born in Hackensack, grew up in Oradell; astronaut; graduated from United States Naval Academy; flew ninety missions during Korean War; test pilot; one of seven original astronauts; flew in *Mercury, Gemini,* and *Apollo* spacecraft

Francis Albert (Frank) Sinatra (1915-   ), born in Hoboken; singer, actor; career launched in 1937 when he won a contest on radio program "Amateur Hour"; immensely popular singer in 1940s; singing led to a Hollywood career as well and he starred in several motion pictures; won Academy Award for best male supporting actor in *From Here to Eternity*; often called "The Voice"

Bruce Springsteen (1949-   ), born in Freehold; musician; one of the most popular rock stars of the late 1970s and the 1980s; began his musical career in the nightclubs along Asbury Park's boardwalk; turned to his New Jersey roots as inspiration for many of his songs; among his albums are *Born to Run, Nebraska,* and *Born in the USA*; nicknamed "The Boss"

John Stevens (1749-1838), long-time resident of Hoboken; lawyer, engineer, inventor; secured legislation that led to establishment of first patent law in United States, 1790; pioneer in the use of steam power; established a steam ferry from Hoboken to New York City; in 1825 built the first American steam locomotive and demonstrated it on a short circular track in Hoboken; in 1830 formed Camden and Amboy Railroad and Transportation Company

Juan Terry Trippe (1899-1981), born in Seabright; businessman; pioneer in establishment of international air travel; in 1927 founded Pan American World Airways

Johnny Vander Meer (1914-   ), born in Prospect Park; professional baseball player; only professional baseball player in history to pitch two no-hitters in a row, which he did in 1938 while playing for the Cincinnati Reds; nicknamed the "Mad Dutchman"

Edward Weston (1850-1936), born in England, settled in Montclair; electrical engineer; founded the Weston Electrical Instrument Company, a leading producer of electrical measuring instruments

Walt Whitman (1819-1892), lived in Camden during the last nineteen years of his life; poet, journalist, essayist; most famous poems, including "When Lilacs Last in the Dooryard Bloom'd," "Song of Myself," and "Captain, My Captain," were published as part of his collection *Leaves of Grass*

William Carlos Williams (1883-1963), born in Rutherford; physician, poet; practiced as a pediatrician for more than forty years; in his autobiography explained that his work as a doctor enriched his writing of poetry: "I was permitted by my medical badge to follow the poor defeated body into those gulfs and grottoes"; his *Paterson* is considered by some to be America's greatest epic poem; won the 1963 Pulitzer Prize in poetry for *Pictures from Breughel*

Thomas Woodrow Wilson (1856-1924), twenty-eighth president of United States; attended Princeton; president of Princeton (1902-10); governor of New Jersey (1911-13); as governor, attacked the state's long-established political corruption, and earned national recognition for his reforms; an idealist who tried unsuccessfully to keep the nation out of World War I; after the war, struggled in vain to have the United States join the League of Nations, a short-lived forerunner of the United Nations; awarded Nobel Peace Prize in 1919; president (1913-21)

John Witherspoon (1723-1794), Presbyterian minister; moved from native Scotland to Princeton in 1768; president of College of New Jersey, now Princeton University (1768-94); outspoken advocate of independence for American colonies; delegate to Continental Congress; only clergyman to sign the Declaration of Independence

JOHN STEVENS

WALT WHITMAN

WM. CARLOS WILLIAMS

WOODROW WILSON

ALEXANDER WOOLCOTT

Alexander Woolcott (1887-1943), born in Phalanx; actor, drama critic, columnist for *New Yorker* magazine

John Woolman (1720-1772), born near Rancocas; clergyman, writer; itinerant Quaker preacher; wrote eloquently against the evils of slavery; helped launch the Abolition movement in America; his *Journal*, published in 1774, is one of the best records we have about everyday colonial life

Patience Lovell Wright (1725-1786), born in Bordentown; sculptor in wax; first American to achieve international fame as a sculptor

GOVERNORS

William Livingston	1776-1790	Leon Abbett	1884-1887
Elisha Lawrence	1790	Robert S. Green	1887-1890
William Paterson	1790-1793	Leon Abbett	1890-1893
Elisha Lawrence	1793	George T. Werts	1893-1896
Richard Howell	1793-1801	John W. Griggs	1896-1898
Joseph Bloomfield	1801-1802	Foster M. Voorhees	1898
John Lambert	1802-1803	David O. Watkins	1898-1899
Joseph Bloomfield	1803-1812	Foster M. Voorhees	1899-1902
Charles Clark	1812	Franklin Murphy	1902-1905
Aaron Ogden	1812-1813	Edward C. Stokes	1905-1908
William S. Pennington	1813-1815	John Franklin Fort	1908-1911
William Kennedy	1815	Woodrow Wilson	1911-1913
Mahlon Dickerson	1815-1817	James E. Fielder	1913
Jesse Upson	1817	Leon R. Taylor	1913-1914
Isaac H. Williamson	1817-1829	James E. Fielder	1914-1917
Garret D. Wall	1829	Walter E. Edge	1917-1919
Peter D. Vroom	1829-1832	William N. Runyon	1919-1920
Samuel L. Southard	1832-1833	Clarence E. Case	1920
Elias P. Seeley	1833	Edward I. Edwards	1920-1923
Peter D. Vroom	1833-1836	George S. Silzer	1923-1926
Philemon Dickerson	1836-1837	A. Harry Moore	1926-1929
William Pennington	1837-1843	Morgan F. Larson	1929-1932
Daniel Haines	1843-1845	A. Harry Moore	1932-1935
Charles C. Stratton	1845-1848	Clifford R. Powell	1935
Daniel Haines	1848-1851	Horace G. Prall	1935
George F. Fort	1851-1854	Harold G. Hoffman	1935-1938
Rodman M. Price	1854-1857	A. Harry Moore	1938-1941
William A. Newell	1857-1860	Charles Edison	1941-1944
Charles S. Olden	1860-1863	Walter E. Edge	1944-1947
Joel Parker	1863-1866	Alfred E. Driscoll	1947-1954
Marcus L. Ward	1866-1869	Robert B. Meyner	1954-1962
Theodore F. Randolph	1869-1872	Richard Hughes	1962-1970
Joel Parker	1872-1875	William T. Cahill	1970-1974
Joseph D. Bedle	1875-1878	Brendan T. Byrne	1974-1982
George B. McClellan	1878-1881	Thomas H. Kean	1982-1990
George C. Ludlow	1881-1884	James Florio	1990-

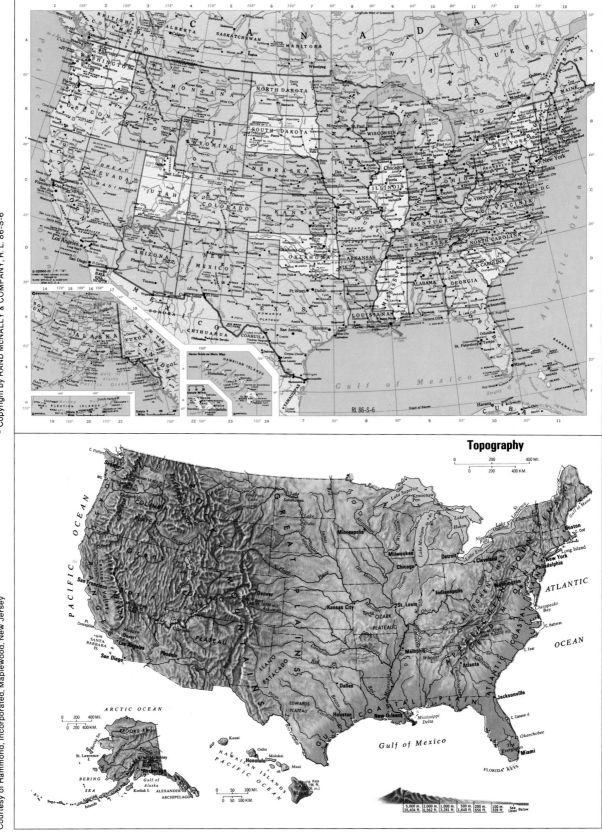

RL 86-S-6

Topography

0   200   400 MI.

0   200   400 KM.

5,000 m. | 2,000 m. | 1,000 m. | 500 m. | 200 m. | 100 m. | Sea | Below
16,404 ft. | 6,562 ft. | 3,281 ft. | 1,640 ft. | 656 ft. | 328 ft. | Level

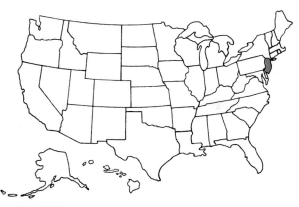

MAP KEY

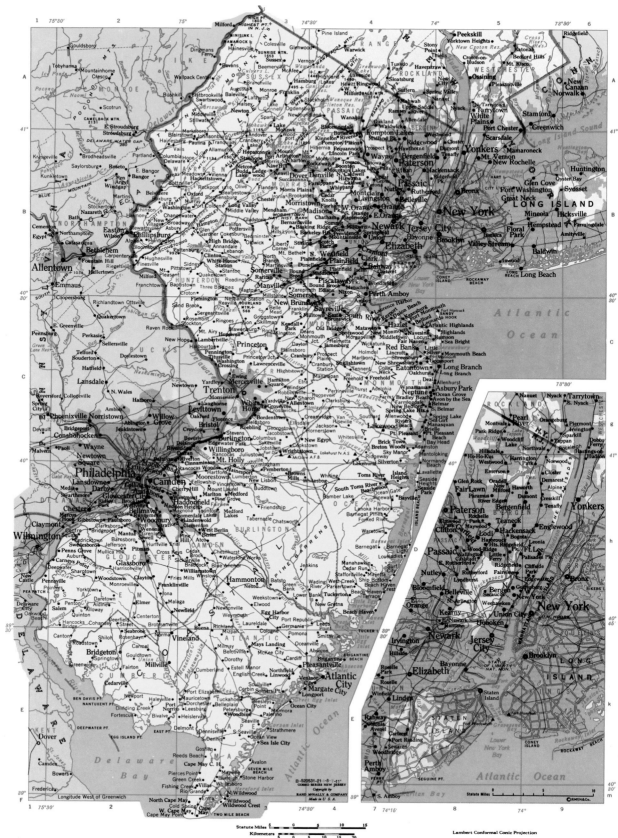

Statute Miles 5 0 5 10 15
Kilometers 5 0 5 10 15 20

Lambert Conformal Conic Projection

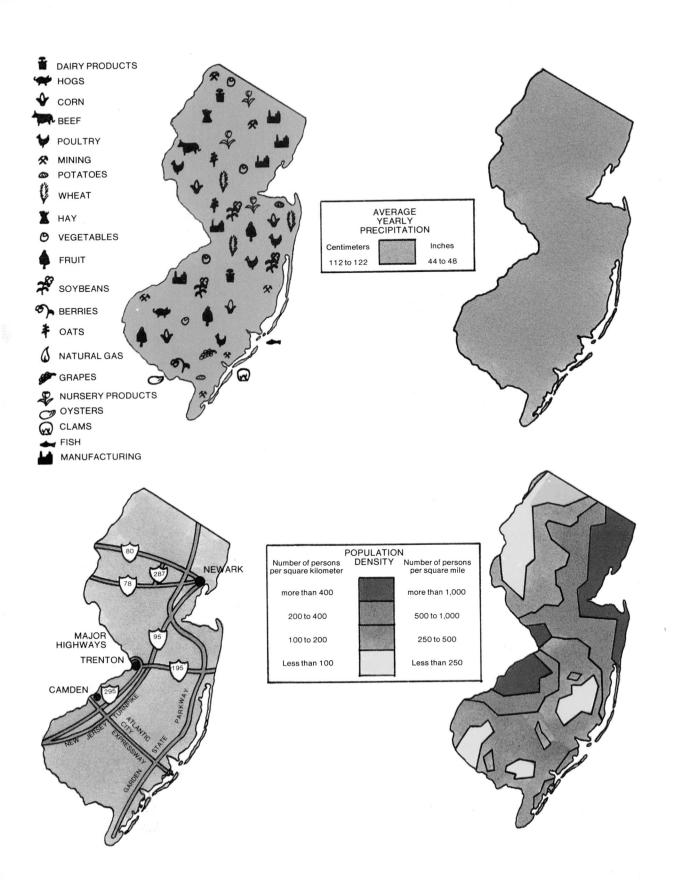

DAIRY PRODUCTS
HOGS
CORN
BEEF
POULTRY
MINING
POTATOES
WHEAT
HAY
VEGETABLES
FRUIT
SOYBEANS
BERRIES
OATS
NATURAL GAS
GRAPES
NURSERY PRODUCTS
OYSTERS
CLAMS
FISH
MANUFACTURING

AVERAGE
YEARLY
PRECIPITATION

Centimeters   Inches

112 to 122   44 to 48

POPULATION
DENSITY
Number of persons   Number of persons
per square kilometer   per square mile

more than 400   more than 1,000

200 to 400   500 to 1,000

100 to 200   250 to 500

Less than 100   Less than 250

MAJOR
HIGHWAYS

NEWARK

TRENTON

CAMDEN

COUNTIES

SUSSEX
• Newton

PASSAIC

BERGEN

WARREN

MORRIS
• Paterson

• Belvidere

• Morristown

• Hackensack

ESSEX
Newark
HUDSON
Jersey
City

UNION
Elizabeth

HUNTERDON

SOMERSET

• Somerville

• Flemington

• New
Brunswick

MIDDLESEX

MERCER
⊛ TRENTON

MONMOUTH
• Freehold

• Mt Holly

• Toms River

BURLINGTON

OCEAN

• Camden

• Woodbury

CAMDEN

GLOUCESTER

SALEM
• Salem

ATLANTIC

• Bridgeton

• Mays Landing

CUMBERLAND

CAPE MAY

• Cape May CH

TOPOGRAPHY

High Point
1,803 ft. (550 m.)

Delaware

KITTATINNY MTS.

Wallkill

Kill

Delaware
Water Gap

Paulins

Musconetcong

SCHOOLEYS MTS.

L.
Hopatcong

Paterson

Hackensack

Passaic

WATCHUNG MTS.

Newark

PALISADES

Jersey
City

Hudson

Round
Valley
Res.

Spruce
Run
Res.

PIEDMONT PLATEAU

Raritan

New
Brunswick

Sandy Hook

Trenton

Millstone

Delaware

Navesink

Long
Branch

Rancocas

Pine

Toms

C
O
A
S
T
A
L

P
L
A
I
N

Camden

Barrens

Mullica

Barnegat B.

Delaware

Gt. Egg Harbor

Cohansey

Maurice

Vineland

Great Bay

Long
Beach

Atlantic
City

Delaware Bay

C. May

Below Sea Level | 100 m. 328 ft. | 200 m. 656 ft. | 500 m. 1,640 ft. | 1,000 m. 3,281 ft. | 2,000 m. 6,562 ft. | 5,000 m. 16,404 ft.

Courtesy of Hammond, Incorporated
Maplewood, New Jersey

Toms River

INDEX

Page numbers that appear in boldface type indicate illustrations

Children pick their own pumpkins at a Branchbury Township farm

Picture Identifications
Front Cover: The Old Red Mill, built in 1763, in Clinton
Back Cover: The beach at Atlantic City
Pages 2-3: Island Beach
Page 6: Colonial Hotel, Cape May
Pages 8-9: A Hunterdon County farm
Page 18: Bathers at Atlantic City
Pages 26-27: "Trading with the Indians"
Page 36: General George Washington at the Battle of Trenton
Page 43: Train in New Jersey
Page 50: The Statue of Liberty
Pages 64-65: The State House, Trenton
Page 78 (inset): Beach scene, Atlantic City
Pages 78-79: Echo Lake Park
Pages 92-93: Brigantine National Wildlife Refuge
Page 93 (inset): Cranberry flotation in the Pinelands
Page 108: Montage showing the state flag, the state tree (red oak), the state flower (purple violet), the state bird (Eastern goldfinch), and the state animal (horse)

About the Author

Deborah Kent grew up in Little Falls, New Jersey. Both of her parents are native-born New Jerseyans, and Ms. Kent was raised on stories about local history. She received a Bachelor of Arts degree in English from Oberlin College, a Masters degree in Social Work from Smith College School for Social Work, and a Master of Fine Arts degree from the University of Guanajuato in Mexico. Ms. Kent worked in a New York City settlement house and taught disabled children in Mexico before she began writing full-time.

Deborah Kent is the author of eleven novels for young adults. This is her first nonfiction book for young readers. She lives in Chicago with her husband and their daughter Janna.

Picture Acknowledgments

H. Armstrong Roberts, Inc.: Pages 5, 18, 43, 50, 78-79, 131 (Whitman); © G. Ahrens: Front cover, pages 4, 2-3, 98, 122; © R. Krubner: Page 20 (left); © E. Degginger: Page 93 (inset)
© **Robert A. Walsh:** Back cover
© **Bob Krist:** Pages 6, 11 (right), 17 (left), 22, 24, 25, 61 (right), 73, 74, 75, 77 (right), 102, 115
© **Jerome Wyckoff:** Pages 11 (left), 12, 20 (right)
© **Mary Ann Brockman:** Pages 8-9, 13, 17 (right), 40, 41, 53 (right), 68 (right), 69, 76, 77 (left), 84, 97, 100, 106, 108 (bottom right), 116, 119
Journalism Services: © Tim McCabe: Page 14 (left)
Nawrocki Stock Photo: © R. Perron: Pages 14, 62; © Jeff Apoian: Page 60; © Peter Panayiotou: Page 61 (left)
Photri: Pages 21, 38, 53, 54, 85, 130 (Pike); © Ira D. Finke: Pages 45, 89, 105 (left); © D. Long: Page 72; © Leonard Lee Rue: Page 108 (bottom left); © Rothstein: Page 113 (left)
Historical Pictures Service, Inc., Chicago: Pages 26-27, 33, 36, 46, 57 (left), 68 (left), 83 (right), 128 (Dodge and Edison), 129 (Frelinghuysen and Kirsten), 130 (Robeson)
The Bettmann Archive: Pages 29, 30, 49, 52, 71, 81, 83, 87 (top), 120, 127 (Burr and Cleveland), 128 (Einstein), 129 (Halsey), 130 (Sinatra), 131 (Williams and Wilson), 132
UPI/Bettmann: Pages 59, 88 (right), 126
Springer/Bettmann Film Archive: Page 87 (bottom)
Library of Congress: Page 31
Tom Stack & Associates: © Imagery: Pages 35, 103; © Joseph Decaro: Page 39
Wide World Photos, Inc.: Pages 55, 57 (right), 64-65, 88 (left), 127 (Bradley and Brooks), 128 (Costello), 129 (Ginsburg), 130 (Springsteen), 131 (Stevens)
© **Pete Taft:** Page 58
© **The Photo Source:** Page 78 (inset), 108 (middle)
Devaney/Gartman Agency: © William R. Wright: Pages 91, 95
Root Resources: © Bill Thomas: Pages 92-93; © Ray F. Hillstrom, Jr.: Page 105 (right);
© James Blank: Page 118
© **Reinhard Brucker:** Page 108 (top right)
© **Cameramann International Ltd.:** Page 110
© **Lynn M. Stone:** Page 113 (right)
Len W. Meents: Maps on pages 95, 97, 100, 103, 136
Courtesy Flag Research Center, Winchester, Massachusetts 01890: Flag on page 108